REFRAMING
POVERTY

D0830573

REFRAMING
POVERTY

New THINKING and FEELING
About Humanity's Greatest Challenge

ERIC MEADE

Reframing Poverty:
New Thinking and Feeling About Humanity's Greatest Challenge
Published by Canyon House Press
Superior, CO

Publisher's Cataloging-in-Publication data

Names: Meade, Eric (1974-), author.
Title: Reframing poverty : new thinking and feeling about humanity's greatest challenge / by Eric Meade.
Description: First trade paperback original edition. | Superior [Colorado] : Canyon House Press, 2019. | Also published as an ebook.
Identifiers: ISBN 978-0-578-42692-1
Subjects: LCSH: Poverty. | Poor.
BISAC: SOCIAL SCIENCE / Poverty.
Classification: LCC HC110.P6 | DDC 339–dc22

Cover design by Victoria Wolf

QUANTITY PURCHASES: Schools, companies, professional groups, clubs, and other organizations may qualify for special terms when ordering quantities of this title. For information, email info@reframingpoverty.com.

"The forward pace of the world which you are pushing will be painfully slow. But what of that: the difference between a hundred and a thousand years is less than you now think. But doing what must be done, that is eternal even when it walks with poverty."

W.E.B. Du Bois

TABLE OF CONTENTS

GRATITUDES

This book's desire to exist is evidenced by the fact that at each point in the writing process, the right person came into my life to offer precisely the help that I needed. These persons include Frederic Laloux, Jessica Hartung, Jonathan Peck, Jennifer Hsu Dearth, Bruce Peters, Les Wallace, Polly Letofsky, Jennifer Jas, and Andrea Costantine. Other friends and mentors, including Richard Weingarten, Doug Krug, and Marty Goldberg, have contributed over the past decade to the thinking within this book.

I am grateful to my students at American University and Watson University, on whom I tested many of these ideas as I formulated them in my own mind. My wife, children, and parents have served as a source of ongoing support and encouragement, as well as critical sounding boards and early reviewers.

In the spirit of the ideas presented later in the book, I would also like to thank Amy Livingston, Arthur McFarlane II, Ben O'Dell, the Bender Library at American University, Bob Tipton, Bob Tomasko, the Boulder Valley Rotary Club, the Colorado Rockies (both the baseball team and the mountain range), Dan Doucette, Dan McCabe, Danny Yaroslavski, Deb Chromik, Derek Bassett, Doug Bernstein, Emily Oehler, Jiang Qingyao, Joan Parker, Kimberly King, Kimberly Pfeifer, Kristen Patterson, Lisa Klesges, the Louisville (Colorado) Public Library, Marakon Associates, Matt Peake, Mylene Huynh, Natalie Burke, Ong'R, Patrick Mellody, Paul's Coffee, Rebecca Saltman, Rex Miller, Shay Holloway, Stephanie Fischer, Sue Williamson, Thomas Laetz, Tim O'Hara, the University of Denver Libraries, the University of Illinois Archives, my father's tenth-grade English teacher, and the young woman at Kramerbooks & Afterwords.

I feel the deepest gratitude toward everyone, whether or not I remembered to mention each name, who has helped this book come into being.

INTRODUCTION

"And because how we feel is intricately tied to how we know, we cannot feel differently if we don't know differently. We need a bigger emotional and cognitive space, one in which we experience that the internal conflicts and inconsistencies of our adaptive challenge are not inevitable and intractable."

Robert Kegan and Lisa Laskow Lahey

The most constructive conversation about poverty may be the one we're not having.

We talk a lot about poverty. Rarely does a day go by without someone offering a new book, white paper, or article marshaling new data to support a particular point of view. Experts make definitive statements on long-standing debates, only to see those debates reopen the next day with a new report issued from the opposing side. The pace of the conversation seems to suggest that we are making daily progress toward understanding – and solving – the problem of poverty.

Unfortunately, most of this conversation is a rehash of the same old views. Contrary to popular opinion, "breakthrough studies" and "radical new perspectives" on poverty are often – for those familiar with the historical discourse – merely rediscoveries of or variations on arguments and proposals heard many times before. The same ideas come and go as seasons and public attitudes change.

But why? Why does so much discussion yield so few genuinely new insights about poverty? The answer is that we have misunderstood the challenge of poverty. We have seen it as a *technical* challenge – one that we can solve once we learn the right skill or methodology. We strive to determine "what works" and to apply it as broadly as possible.

Too bad it's not that simple. We cannot have a straightforward, technical discussion about poverty because the topic is too emotionally charged, and for good reason. Until recently, the vast majority of humans were poor. A mere 200 years ago, 83.9 percent of humans lived in extreme poverty, on less than $1 per day (in 1985 dollars)[1], which is roughly equivalent (accounting for inflation) to the World Bank's poverty threshold today. Poverty is the ground from which most of us who are not poor have only recently emerged. Most of us would only have to look back a couple of generations to find a relative who genuinely struggled to survive. How our own relatives made it out of poverty – or why they were unable to do so – likely shapes how we think and feel about poverty today.

Thus, poverty is not just a *technical* challenge. In the words of Robert Kegan and Lisa Laskow Lahey as quoted above, poverty is an "adaptive challenge." It requires us to change not just what we do but also who we are. It requires us to change how we think and how we feel, and to work through the emotions we carry forward from our personal and familial experiences of poverty. Only then can we shift the focus from the unresolved needs of our own pasts to what the world needs from us right now.

Prior to that shift, we experience "internal conflicts and inconsistencies." In our dealings with *others*, we cling to our own limited ideas about poverty at the expense of the ideas of others, preventing meaningful collaboration and partnership. In our dealings with *the poor*, we unconsciously project the difficulties of our own lives, and we offer the poor not what they need but what we feel fulfilled in providing. In our dealings with *ourselves*, we reject new insights and discoveries that threaten our established identities and our ways of understanding the world.

After we work through our emotions about poverty, however, we become more potent leaders of change. In our dealings with *others*, we embrace multiple perspectives to build collaborative partnerships with those we previously may have avoided. In our dealings with *the poor*, we respond to their most pressing needs rather than making them foils for our own challenges. In our dealings with *ourselves*, we recognize that the emotions poverty evokes in us may actually raise issues we need to address in our own lives.

These benefits accrue not only to those who address poverty on a professional or volunteer basis, but also to all who are concerned about the state of their own communities. The question we must address affects each one of us. It is not: *How do we eradicate poverty?* But rather it is: *What am I, as a human being, to do, living as I do in a world where poverty exists?* This question demands a new conversation – one in which we look deeply into our own experiences.

This book opens the door to that conversation. Part One explores what our society has already been saying about poverty, but in a novel way. First, it shows how our emotions about poverty shape how we think about it. Second, it explores the range of perspectives on poverty and suggests the emotions that may be associated with each. Finally, it concludes that all such perspectives have some validity.

Part Two reframes those perspectives by introducing concepts not currently included in the poverty conversation. These concepts allow for a way of thinking about poverty in which all the major perspectives can be true at the same time. They also highlight and address areas where I believe the poverty conversation overall has heretofore fallen short.

Throughout the book, I will offer a series of nested insights drawn from my own experience living in developing countries, consulting to nonprofits, teaching social enterprise classes at the university level, serving on the board of a global development non-governmental organization (NGO), and otherwise living my unique human life. What you will do with these insights, I cannot say. What I *can* say is that after reading this book, you will be able to enter into a new, more constructive conversation about poverty.

PART ONE

CHAPTER ONE

HOW WE FEEL SHAPES WHAT WE THINK

"Emotions ... lead organisms to act as if certain things were true about the present circumstances, whether or not they are, because they were true of past circumstances. ... In this lies their strength and their weakness ..."

John Tooby and Leda Cosmides

In a radio interview on May 23, 2017, U.S. Secretary of Housing and Urban Development Ben Carson said this about poverty:

> I think poverty to a large extent is also a state of mind. You take somebody that has the right mindset, you can take everything from them and put them on the street, and I guarantee in a little while they'll be right back up there. You take somebody with the wrong mindset, you can give them everything in the world – they'll work their way right back down to the bottom.[1]

Carson's comments provoked outrage on the part of anti-poverty activists. Hunger Free America CEO Joel Berg retorted,

"Overwhelming facts and data prove that the main causes of poverty are low wages, too few jobs, and an inadequate safety net – not some sort of personal attitude problem."[2]

In a letter to *The New York Times*, Elizabeth Arend from the National Council for Behavioral Health wrote, "Statements like this by Mr. Carson ... encapsulate ... a fundamental belief that some people are inherently worthy, and the rest are not," adding that generations of politicians have used this point of view to deny essential services to poor Americans "while ignoring racism, gender discrimination and other institutionalized drivers of poverty."[3]

Olivia Golden, executive director of the nonpartisan Center for Law and Social Policy (CLASP), said that Carson's [alleged] suggestion that poor people are lazy or somehow at fault is "an idea that through American history has been an excuse for really bad policy decisions."[4]

On the conservative Fox News television show *Tucker Carlson Tonight*, however, a panel reached a different conclusion. Former Democratic political operative David "Mudcat" Saunders said, "I think freeloading [that is, living off the efforts of others] is a state of mind, but I think that poverty is real, at least where I live in southwest Virginia." Black conservative commentator Crystal Wright added:

> Freeloading's real ... What Carson's talking about is, if you keep thinking, well I'm gonna be poor, and I can always reach out to the government, take care of me, there's really no incentive there to rise up and work. You can't blink yourself out of poverty, but you can have a state of mind that says, "You know what? I'm gonna work myself out of poverty."[5]

Cornell University human ecology professor Gary Evans agreed that there may be a poverty mindset, but suggested that poverty *causes* the mindset. "There's definitely evidence that poverty – particularly childhood poverty – does affect things like persistence, your executive functioning [in the brain], your ability to control attention, to inhibit emotions."[6]

Further, the stresses of poverty contribute to behaviors that can keep a person poor, like not weeding one's fields or not saving for the future. According to Princeton University behavioral scientist Eldar Shafir, "All the data shows it isn't about poor people, it's about people who happen to be in poverty. All the data suggests it is not the person, it's the context they're inhabiting."[7]

Carson's comments align with the idea that there is a "culture of poverty" – that is, a coherent set of attitudes and behaviors that perpetuates poverty across generations. Developed by anthropologist Oscar Lewis[8] in the 1950s, this idea influenced the War on Poverty launched in 1964 by President Lyndon Johnson. But the political left later rejected it as "blaming the victim,"[9] and the political right used it (often in a racialized form targeting African-Americans) to scale back social assistance programs.

The forty-eight hours after Carson's interview saw a reprise of four distinct explanations for poverty – that it is caused by:

- The mindset of the poor.
- A lack of opportunity.
- A lack of personal responsibility.
- The stress effects of being poor.

There is nothing new under the sun. All four of these perspectives have been around for a long time, coming in and out of fashion as public sentiments change. Even the stress effects of being poor highlighted by Evans and Shafir are not fundamentally new, though their support from brain science is a recent addition to the thinking.

But why the ongoing debate? If one of these four perspectives is correct and the others are incorrect, as the promoters of each seem to believe, then why have we not yet settled the question? Why do multiple views persist in parallel – and even in conflict with one another? Why have we not been able to integrate them into a broader theory that everyone can accept? Why do we still not know for sure what causes poverty?

We need to step back and look at the overall question of whether poverty has causes. Poverty is the initial condition of the human species; it has been here as long as we have. Most of our ancestors lived "hand to mouth," foraging for nuts and berries, hunting for game, or farming small plots of land. This state of affairs continued even into the lifetimes of ancestors whose names we know. Poverty exists without cause; it is the ground from which we humans have been evolving.

For most of human existence, however, no one spoke of poverty. Most humans probably thought nothing of it when they saw someone who was struggling to survive, since they were struggling just as hard themselves. That struggle was not called "poverty"; it was called "life."

It was not until some humans were *not* poor that they could even conceptualize such a thing as poverty. Once the newly non-poor had the leisure to think beyond their own survival, they turned their attention to others they described as living in poverty. Even today, as economist John Kenneth Galbraith notes, "In many societies the poor [may] react to their economic situation with less anxiety than do the rich."[10] In isolated communities, the poor may not even know they are poor.

It seems, then, that poverty as a construct has less to do with a certain set of life circumstances caused by a certain set of factors than it does with the effect those circumstances have on an observer – that is, the emotions it evokes. These emotions shape the discourse on poverty, including its attribution to one set of causes or another. Poverty is, at its root, an emotional construct.

This is not how we typically speak of poverty. We define poverty as an objective construct – as living below a certain income level deemed necessary to acquire life's necessities ($1.90 a day according to the World Bank,[11] $12,140 a year according to the U.S. government[12]) or as a confluence of multiple social, economic, and political challenges (as in the UN's Multidimensional Poverty Index[13]). We map it to concepts like inequality, injustice, or vulnerability that we can define and measure in the real world. From the tone of the conversation, one would think we have no emotions about poverty at all.

But we do. These impersonal constructs disguise a conversation that is deeply personal for all of us, since we all have a connection to poverty. Some of us have been poor ourselves, either in the absolute sense of lacking food, money, or housing, or in the relative sense of lacking resources or opportunities that seem to come easily to others. Others of us have not experienced poverty directly, but we have a connection to it through those we love.

This is my own situation. I am a white, middle-class American man with a master's degree who has never been poor by any established standard. Even when I have been low on cash, I have always known that I could rely on the financial support of my family.

But my father was raised poor in rural upstate New York, where he lived at various times in a subsidized apartment, a

trailer with no running water, and a house that had original-
ly been built as a garage. His father was one-quarter Native
American and worked as a manual laborer, and his mother was
a white woman who left school at age sixteen to work as a domestic servant to help her family make ends meet during the
Great Depression. My father was the first in his family to join
the middle class, and the only one in his generation.

My wife grew up poor as well. She was raised in a small
Chinese village until the age of eleven, when she was selected
for a special "prodigy class" at the boarding school in a nearby
city. Her parents had grown up during Mao Zedong's Great
Leap Forward, in which tens of millions died of famine. They
started their family during the Cultural Revolution a decade or
so later. My father-in-law was a schoolteacher and my mother-
in-law self-studied to become a Chinese herbal doctor.

I suspect that many rich and middle-class people are connected to poverty in ways similar to mine. Given how recently
the majority of humans were poor, it is likely that most of us
can find a fairly recent experience of poverty with just a peek
into our family histories or social networks. The experiences of
those we love, as well as our relationships with them, continue
to shape our thoughts and feelings about poverty today.

Even those with no known familial connection to poverty
still carry the experiences of their ancestors. Poverty is the context in which we have evolved as a species. It lives on in our
brain structures and in our relationships, whether we know it
or not. Some of the emotions we feel every day started out as
survival mechanisms for the ordeals we faced as early humans
living in conditions we would now describe as poverty.

Further, our ancestral legacy of living in small bands, in
which each member's survival depended on that of the entire

group, embedded in us a deep concern for the well-being of others. Even a brief encounter with poverty, like walking past a homeless person in the street, can bring this concern to the surface. A flood of feelings and sensations tells us that the situation is important; it touches something deep within us. For all these reasons, poverty is not something we can discuss without emotion.

If poverty is an emotional construct, then it requires an emotional definition so that we are all talking about the same thing. For the purposes of our own analyses, we can each set our own thresholds of what constitutes poverty to us, but if we want to talk about poverty together we need a definition that describes what is common across all such thresholds. We need a definition of poverty that captures the emotions we feel about it.

I propose the following:

> *Poverty is a sustained level of deprivation on the part of a human or group of humans that evokes a significant emotional response on the part of an observer.*

Since this is a novel way to define poverty, a few explanatory notes are in order.

Typically, we speak of poverty only with respect to humans. While we may show concern for a stray or starved animal, it would be quite unusual to say that the animal lives in poverty.

Deprivation refers here to the lack of something that the observer considers necessary for a human being to live an adequate life. This deprivation could take any form: food, shelter, internet access, whatever. Assessments of what is necessary to live vary according to context, time, and perspective. This accounts for differences in official poverty levels from one country to the next, and for the ever-expanding definitions of poverty used by international organizations like the UN. Poverty is inherently relative.

The word "sustained" indicates that the deprivation is a persistent feature of the person's life rather than a temporary inconvenience or a choice. Thus, we can exclude from our discussion middle-class college students supported by their parents and "starving artists" who sacrifice financial security for artistic purposes.

The word "emotional" is a bit harder to tackle. Like poverty, it has eluded precise definition, but scientists generally agree that it involves neural circuits and physiological responses (elevated heart rate, sweaty palms) that, upon recognizing something in the environment (which could include one's own thoughts), produce an inner state that mobilizes the organism to take a particular type of action.[14]

You may initially reject a definition of poverty in terms of the emotions felt by an observer who is not even poor. This is the component of the definition with which people seem to have the most difficulty. My point is not that people do not know for themselves that they are suffering, but rather that what brings their situation into a conversation about poverty is the broader recognition by others that their material lack has reached a level that is significant, as measured by their emotional response to it. Conversely, even critics would probably agree that if someone cannot find any observer who agrees that they are poor, then they probably aren't. In any event, the purpose of this definition is not to give some people status over others in terms of the severity of their suffering, but rather to highlight the fundamentally emotional nature of our experience of poverty.

You may say, "Poverty *is* a single mother who cannot

provide for her child," or, "Poverty *is* someone not being able to access medical treatment for a life-threatening illness."

I do not deny that those are incredibly difficult situations. I am just saying that it confuses the conversation when we define poverty in strictly objective terms, when we try to leave our emotions out. Further, we are mostly unsuccessful in doing so. A quick exercise should make this clear.

If you felt the initial resistance I mentioned above, then I invite you to call to mind whatever image represents what poverty is to you. When you hold that image in your mind, what emotions come to the fore? How do you feel? What sensations do you have in your body? Do you feel strongly that you must *do something*? My guess is that your emotions at calling this image to mind are strong, which may be why this image seems to you an undeniable manifestation of poverty. You may now want to ask yourself:

- Why does this image evoke such strong emotions?
- How do these emotions shape my response to the issue described?
- How does the image relate to my own life and experience?

If you can meaningfully explore these questions, then perhaps the above definition of poverty has already begun to show its value.

That said, defining poverty in terms of the experience of the observer who is not poor certainly goes against the recent trend of trying to give voice to the poor themselves. For example, a 2000 project of the World Bank, *Voices of the Poor: Can Anyone Hear Us?*, sought to capture personal narratives of the poor.[15] The trend has clearly been toward lifting up the voices of the poor themselves, even to the point of discounting the opinions of those with no direct, personal experience of poverty.

But we must be careful here. First, even the desire to give voice to the poor, while on the face of it noble and appropriate, may itself be an emotional projection. Those in rich countries who feel their own voices have been ignored in the past will likely – once they engage in poverty work – emphasize giving voice to the poor, and particularly the poor who are most like them. The power dynamics that squelch the poor may trigger feelings about power dynamics they experience in their own lives. Thus triggered, they may act in ways that play out their own feelings but do not necessarily serve the best interests of the poor.

Second, the emotions of the non-poor shape how they hear what the poor have to say. It is difficult even in our most intimate relationships to hear other human beings without filtering what they say through our own emotions and attachments. How much more difficult this must be with respect to people from different communities or countries and with vastly different life experiences!

This is important because the non-poor make many of the big decisions that shape the lives of the poor. Their emotions have real impacts on the poor. They drive policy and programs. They perpetuate the intractable debate among ostensibly objective perspectives. They shape how individual people conceptualize poverty, which in turn shapes what they are likely to do (and not do) about it.

To define poverty in emotional terms is to recognize its significance for all of us and to set the foundation for the most constructive conversation we could possibly have about it.

∞

Twenty-five-year-old Amber McGuffy[16] is a mother to three girls, ages seven, five, and two. The girls all have different fathers. Amber lives in a subsidized, two-bedroom apartment in rural Pennsylvania, where she works in a high school cafeteria. Several years ago, she married a man, but he became physically abusive, so she left him and a local women's shelter helped to support her.

Like her own daughters, Amber was raised in poverty by a single mother. When she was fourteen, Amber entered foster care due to her mother's opioid addiction. She has not heard from her mother in years. Before finishing high school, she attended twenty-three different schools as she was shuffled from home to home. Remarkably, a college accepted her with a full scholarship, but she gave it up that summer when she discovered she was pregnant.

Amber has managed to make ends meet with a combination of social services and low-wage jobs. She participated in a government work training program to become a certified nurse assistant but has been unable to find a job because she has no transportation. Two weeks after she finished the program, a hit-and-run driver totaled her car while it was parked outside her apartment. Getting a higher-paying job would have downsides anyway, since she would lose her paid child care and would have to pay most of her increase in income to a babysitter.

∞

Robert Hanga[17] lives near the main road in his village in Tanzania. He has five children between the ages of four and twenty whom he has been raising on his own since his wife's death during the birth of his youngest daughter. Robert is

HIV-positive, as are his two youngest children. They receive anti-retroviral therapy (ART) through a local clinic funded by an international NGO.

Robert makes a living primarily by growing potatoes on his small plot and selling them to itinerant agents who bring the goods to the city, and most of the time they come back to make payment once they sell the goods. Robert is known as a good neighbor and a hard worker. He often earns extra money by doing small carpentry projects in a nearby town.

Robert's oldest daughter left school to help her father with the other children after her mother died. Robert has always told his children that they must finish school, but more practical needs have taken priority. Recently he took his sixteen-year-old son out of school so his son could help him on a construction project in town.

∞

Books about poverty typically include stories like these. Often the stories set up the arguments that the author would like to make regarding what is wrong with the situation, how it came to be, and what should be done about it. You may already be considering these questions yourself with respect to Amber or Robert. If so, then I invite you to take a deep breath and contemplate a different question instead.

How do you *feel* when you read these two stories?

- You may feel angry, for example, at an economic system that allows such poverty to persist, or at the men who have fathered Amber's children but shoulder no responsibility, or at the agents who fail to pay Robert for his potatoes.

- You may feel sad that Amber had such a difficult child-hood, or that Robert's wife lost her life while giving birth to their daughter.
- You may feel disgusted with Amber's multiple preg-nancies out of wedlock, or with Robert's decision to take his son out of school.
- You may feel guilty that you have had it so easy – that you have never had to deal with the challenges Amber and Robert have faced.
- If you were raised in poverty like Amber or Robert, you may feel proud that you have somehow managed to cre-ate a better life for yourself.
- You may feel something else altogether.

All these emotions are perfectly natural and valid. Emotions are *inherently* valid. They reflect our own past experiences and they have something important to tell us about our environment or about ourselves, even when they are not appropriate for the situation that evoked them.

Where do these emotions come from?

Many scientists view emotions as evolutionarily adaptive responses to fundamental life tasks performed by humans go-ing back to our earliest ancestors.[18] This explains why some emotions are universal – they have proven necessary for hu-man survival in all contexts. Fear prompts you to run from a predator. Anger prepares you to fight back. Disgust tells you that a certain slab of meat is rancid and you should not eat it. If you felt a particular emotion when reading one of the stories above, then it may be that something in that story triggered the "theme" associated with that emotion (e.g., the theme for sad-ness is loss).

Your emotion may reflect a memory from earlier in your

own life, particularly if you have experienced situations similar in some respect to those described. Your emotions may also relate to events in your parents' or grandparents' lives that took place before you were even born that they passed on to you as unconscious beliefs about the world. For example, if you learned early on that women should abstain from sex until marriage, or that fathers cannot be trusted, then these beliefs will likely prompt a corresponding emotional response when you hear stories about others' lives. Wherever they come from, our emotions affect what we do, how we perceive, and even how we think.

How we feel affects what we do. Psychologist Paul Ekman has created a website that demonstrates this for a lay audience by presenting a situation where a friend gets angry with you. If you feel anger, you may argue with your friend. If you feel afraid, you may imagine your friend leaving you. If you feel disgust, you may belittle your friend. If you feel sad, you may be ashamed. If you feel enjoyment, then you may gloat.[19] The same external event can provoke all these actions, depending on your emotion.

How we feel affects how we perceive. Depending on your emotional state, you will see yourself in different situations in the real world. The emotion reinforces this perception by limiting the information you can take in and by selecting information consistent with the kind of situation your neural circuits have identified and for which the emotion you feel is appropriate. This is particularly true during what Ekman calls the "refractory" period, when the emotion is at its strongest.[20]

How we feel affects how we think. As you become consciously aware of what is happening, you may start to notice information that suggests your initial emotional response was out of place. For example, you may realize that your friend is not really attacking you or that she is not really going to abandon you. You may decide to recalibrate your response based on the new information.

Or you may not. You may decide to ignore the new information and create a story that justifies the emotion you felt initially, whether or not that story is true. You may project a malicious intent onto your friend's behavior to justify the hurtful things you said in response, or you may think of other times when your friend abandoned you, so you can establish a pattern – even if she was not abandoning you *this* time. You may make up this story on the spot or you may import the "script" of a situation that has given you trouble in the past.[21] This is how emotions shape our understanding of the world around us. Rationality is a subset of emotionality. We feel first, and then we create a story that justifies our having felt that way.

Imagine now that we replace Ekman's example of a friend getting mad at you with a face-to-face encounter with Amber or Robert, whom we met earlier. How do you feel in that encounter, and what might those feelings predispose you to do?

- If you feel guilty, then you may try to dispense with your guilt by offering Amber financial help, or by setting up an online donation to an NGO that is active in Tanzania. Guilt will focus your attention on the people who could have treated Amber or Robert better, but didn't.
- If you feel angry, then you may have the urge to punish those you see as culpable, such as the foster care system in the U.S. (e.g., by advocating for reform) or the government of Tanzania (e.g., through public shaming of corrupt officials). You will notice other situations where these institutions have not provided the services for which they were intended.

- If you feel disgust, then you may urge your elected leaders to cut the social programs and foreign aid programs that direct money toward the poor. You may accumulate evidence of cases where the poor have manipulated or defrauded these programs.

- If you feel proud that you have escaped poverty, then you may want to solidify your new middle-class identity by offering Amber advice or by hosting a fundraiser for a charity in Tanzania. Pride will direct your attention to the tangible signs of how far you have come in your own life.

You may then come across new information suggesting that your initial emotional response to Amber or Robert was out of place. If you feel disgust, for example, you may discover that Amber is doing the best she can or that the school Robert's son is leaving provides little in the way of education anyway. Then you have a choice. You can either let go of the emotion that ultimately proved out of place or you can make up a story as to why it was appropriate after all. If you choose the latter, you may tell yourself that Amber was only being nice to get a handout, or that Robert never really supported his children's education anyway.

When the stories we create to justify an emotion come to define our understanding of the world, we have moved from an emotion to a mood. While an *emotion* will come and go relatively quickly in response to a specific stimulus, people in a *mood* are saturated with the trappings of an emotion over a longer period of time. Their moods shape the stories they make up to explain what they observe around them, and these stories take on a life of their own. Because they are particularly alert to events that might trigger that emotion, they find such events whenever they occur. In the popular animated film *Inside Out*, the five emotions of anger, fear, disgust, sadness, and joy are present inside each character's head, but in each case, only one of them is in charge.[22] That one represents the character's mood, his or her prevailing default emotional state.

For example, if you feel anger not just toward Amber's past boyfriends but toward all men, then your anger may be more mood than emotion. If you feel disgust not only about Amber's out-of-wedlock pregnancies but about anyone you feel is settling for less than they could achieve, then your disgust may be a mood. If you feel guilt around people who have what you have, as much as you feel guilt around those who do not, then perhaps your guilt is a mood rather than just an emotion – you may simply feel that you do not deserve what you have.

In this way, people in different moods notice different information in the same narrative – and based on that information, they weave their own explanations for what they have heard. While we tend to assume that our understanding of a situation is based on the facts, and that only later do we feel an emotion about it, the causality often runs in the opposite direction. Based on our moods, we create self-justifying mental models that support – and reinforce – how we already feel.

This explains why we attribute poverty, which as the initial condition of the human species cannot have causes *per se*, to so many factors – e.g., lack of opportunity, lack of personal responsibility, psychological stresses, the wrong mindset. The factors to which we attribute causation are determined in large part by the emotion or mood of the person making the attribution. Since the disagreements among these views are based not on facts and evidence but on emotion, efforts to craft an integrated perspective on poverty prove fruitless.

These dynamics play out even on a global scale. According to John Kenneth Galbraith, newfound concern over poor countries after World War II led first to an action, and then to a theory that justified that action, whether or not it was true. After the World Bank provided technical assistance and capital to poor countries, it elaborated a theory of poverty in which the absence of technical assistance and capital was the problem. As Galbraith notes:

> ... in the great explosion of concern over poverty, we did not ... move from cause to remedy; we moved from the only available line of remedial action to the cause that called for that action.[23]

Galbraith adds that over subsequent decades, society consistently identified the cause of poverty as the lack of whatever it was the donor country had to offer – a pattern that justified the emotions and the actions of the rich.

Even hard data cannot help us see through our own stories. In 2015, the World Bank undertook a study of how ideological and political outlooks affect its staff's interpretation of new data. Researchers provided one data set, labeled in two different ways, and asked two different questions. First, which of two skin creams was more effective, and second, whether minimum wage laws reduce poverty. Staff were more likely to answer correctly for the question about the skin creams than about wage laws, even though both questions used the same data.[24]

We all have our stories about poverty – explanations that support the emotions and moods that we have about it, or that we have about life in general. We can consider explanations of poverty not only as statements to weigh objectively against the evidence, but also as a vocabulary to express how the person providing the explanation feels about poverty. We all have emotionally rich experiences of poverty, whether ancestral, familial, or personal, and these experiences come out in how we explain poverty in the world.

We can see this in Ben Carson's comments about a "poverty mindset" and in the responses those comments provoked. Attributing poverty to low wages and a lack of jobs may reveal anger. Blaming the "freeloading" behavior of the poor may indicate disgust or contempt. Ben Carson, who was himself raised poor in Detroit before achieving renown as a neurosurgeon, may have been expressing pride in his own accomplishments by describing the destructive mindset he left behind.

Of course, these are just suggestions; there is no one-to-one mapping between emotions and explanations. People will travel from emotion to explanation through the unique territories of their own lived experiences. So, the intent here is not to psychoanalyze anyone in particular but rather to invite everyone into a discussion of how our emotions shape our views on poverty, since when we ignore these emotions we create suffering.

First, we suffer because we keep having the same conversation over and over again without touching what is really going on. We even spend a fair amount of time debating what to *call* the poor: the poor, people experiencing poverty, the impoverished, the vulnerable, etc.

As we all know, a conversation between two people that leaves the underlying emotions unaddressed is unlikely to surface the actions necessary to resolve the issue. If that is true for the mundane details of a single relationship (e.g., a married couple), then how much more so for something as universally significant as poverty? By naming our emotions about poverty, we get to the heart of the matter and reach the deeper issues that we must resolve.

Second, we suffer when we cling to our own limited understanding of poverty and when we deny (even to ourselves) evidence of opposing opinions that deep down we know must be true. When presented with a study showing that employers receiving two equivalent resumes for a job are more likely to reject the candidate with an African-American-sounding name,[25] even the evangelist of personal responsibility must admit – at least to herself – that racial discrimination remains a factor in economic success. When presented with stories of poor people who lost good jobs based on their own derelict behavior, even the decrier of economic injustice must accept – at least in his own thoughts – that the poor often make bad decisions. But when we refuse to acknowledge this evidence so that we can preserve an artifice we know to be false, we incur a large psychological cost. We stand on shaky ground and we know it.

Third, we suffer because our limited understanding of poverty produces limited action to address it. Our efforts often fail to achieve their desired objectives or – worse – produce even greater problems in the future. In some cases, we may work against the improvements we sought to effect. And to cap it all off, when we fail we may even blame those we were trying to help for not behaving as our limited understanding had led us to believe they would.

The costs of this suffering suggest the value of exploring *why* we each see poverty as we do – through limited explanations that project our own emotions and experiences. As we detach from those views, we may see that other perspectives have something to offer as well. We can then build a broader and larger understanding of poverty that includes what is useful about each perspective. Then we can take a step toward resolving our inner conflicts and we can strengthen our efforts to help the poor, perhaps with new partners or through new actions we previously would not have considered.

What do people say about poverty, and why?

CHAPTER TWO

STORIES WE MAKE UP ABOUT POVERTY

"It is painful to accept fully the simple fact that one begins from where one is, that one must break free of the web of illusions one spins about life."

Saul D. Alinsky

In the previous chapter, I defined poverty in emotional terms and suggested that we should view many of the explanations we come up with for poverty not just as objective assertions about reality, but also as a vocabulary for expressing how we feel about poverty. If we can work through the emotions that bind us to one explanation over all others, then we can combine what is true about *each* explanation into a broader theory of poverty that informs new, more potent action to reduce it. But first, we need to get a handle on the range of explanations that people have proposed, and why. This chapter introduces and applies a framework for doing so.

We can use a two-by-two matrix to arrange Ben Carson's comments about a poverty mindset and the responses those comments provoked, and show how people choose to approach the issue of poverty with different sets of assumptions.

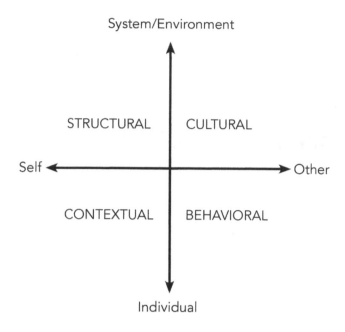

System/Environment

STRUCTURAL | CULTURAL

Self ← → Other

CONTEXTUAL | BEHAVIORAL

Individual

Figure 1.

As seen in **Figure 1**, the horizontal axis captures the relationship of the observer to the person being observed. On the left-hand side, the observer views the person experiencing poverty as fundamentally like them – that is, as a "self." On the right-hand side, the observer sees the poor person as fundamentally different from them – as an "other."

The vertical axis shows the relationship of the person experiencing poverty to the environment, in the opinion of the observer. The observer may believe that poverty is fundamentally a function of the "individual" or of the "system" or "environment."

Ben Carson's comments belong in the upper-right quadrant, where poor people are seen as an "other," since they have a mindset that differs qualitatively from the observer's, and where poverty is a product of the broader cultural environment that fosters or perpetuates that mindset.[1] Here poverty is viewed as a *cultural* (or *subcultural* within a broader society) failure. Other perspectives in this quadrant include the "culture of poverty" mentioned earlier, the "tangle of pathology" described in the 1965 "Moynihan Report" (*The Negro Family: A Case for National Action*),[2] and – to a certain extent – research on the parenting styles of the poor.

The term "freeloading" places the Fox News panel squarely in the lower-right quadrant, where people view poverty as a *behavioral* failure. Freeloading, or shirking one's responsibilities and living off the efforts of others, indicates an individual failure of motivation or work ethic. The poor persons may have the capacity to make better decisions; they just choose not to.

The "freeloaders" are viewed as "other," since they lack the observer's (implicitly self-proclaimed) sense of personal responsibility. Saunders's distinction between the genuine poverty in his hometown in southwest Virginia (among people like him) and the freeloading that occurs elsewhere (among people different from him) reinforces this point.

In the upper-left quadrant are Carson's liberal critics who view poverty as a *structural* failure caused by unemployment, institutional racism, gender inequity, and the like. People here essentially view poor people as like them ("self") and they see poverty as a systems-level phenomenon. As Democratic congresswoman Nita Lowey of New York tweeted:

States of mind: Happy. Sad. New York.
Not a state of mind: Systemic poverty.[3]

Behavioral scientists like Evans and Shafir dwell in the lower-left quadrant, where poverty is a *contextual* failure. The stresses of poverty promote decision-making that keeps people in poverty. These stresses include the "bandwidth tax" that reduces cognitive capacity by up to fourteen IQ points, and the "decision fatigue" that sets in when the financial stakes are so high that every decision requires an exhausting degree of thought and attention.

The observer in this quadrant views the poor as "self." In fact, behavioral scientists argue that the non-poor face the same stresses in other situations where their own resources are scarce, as in the case of a professional manager with limited time but much to do. The difference with poverty is simply that the stakes are far greater and that the poor have less freedom to make lifestyle changes to alleviate the stresses.

Let us now explore each of these quadrants so we can understand the full scope of explanations that people have offered, and so we can consider the emotions that may lie beneath them. Of course, this review will not capture *everything* that anyone has ever said about poverty. Informed readers will no doubt think of other authors and ideas that we could include in one or another of the quadrants. I will simply give a flavor of each of the four explanations introduced above and identify the key variants. I will not proceed chronologically to follow the evolution of the poverty discourse, largely because I am more struck by what has not changed than by what has.

∞

Poverty results from bad decisions or behaviors that put or keep a person in poverty. So claim adherents of the *behavioral* explanation of poverty. But what does this mean? What specific decisions and behaviors bring about poverty, and why do poor people engage in those decisions and behaviors?

For the U.S., researchers Ron Haskins and Isabel Sawhill have identified a basic "success sequence" consisting of finishing high school, working full time at a job, and marrying before having children.[4] They note that:

> Individuals in families headed by an able-bodied adult between the ages of twenty-five and sixty-four have a 98 percent chance of escaping poverty if the family adheres to all three social norms. By contrast, 76 percent of those living in families that do not adhere to any of these norms are poor.[5]

The problem, then, is that many people do not stay on this straight and narrow path to middle-class life. This leaves it to hard-working, tax-paying citizens to foot the bill.

But why do the poor not take on the behaviors, such as working at a job, that so demonstrably and consistently lift people out of poverty? The simplest explanation, according to the *behavioral* view, is that they choose not to. They lack "personal responsibility," which to Haskins and Sawhill "means that individuals must make decisions and take actions that promote their own growth and well-being as well as that of their children."[6]

In his memoir of growing up poor in the American "Rust Belt," J.D. Vance describes a co-worker at a tile warehouse who was chronically late and took bathroom breaks up to an hour long. Vance describes:

> ... a young man with every reason to work – a
> wife-to-be and a baby on the way – carelessly
> tossing aside a good job with excellent health in-
> surance. More troublingly, when it was all over,
> he thought something had been done *to him*.
> There is a lack of agency here – a feeling that you
> have little control over your life and a willing-
> ness to blame everyone but yourself.[7]

It seems that some people may be poor because they lack the basic motivation to improve their own lives.

Alternatively, the poor may be sufficiently motivated but may lack the innate talents necessary for economic success. Three notable expressions of this view over the last few centuries come to mind. The first, popular in the late 19th century, applied Darwin's theory of evolution to poverty and other social phenomena – a school of thought called Social Darwinism. This view held that humans, like other species, followed the law of "survival of the fittest," and that the poorer elements of human society reflected a "residuum" of lower-grade specimens who were not fit but had not yet died off.

However, British scholar John Welshman, in his review of the historical discourse on the so-called "underclass," concludes that this application of Darwin's ideas was not meant to imply that the poor were unable to change. As economics luminary Alfred Marshall writes:

> Those who have been called the Residuum of our
> large towns have little opportunity for friend-
> ship; they know nothing of the decencies and the
> quiet, and very little even of the unity of family

life; and religion fails to reach them. No doubt their physical, mental, and moral ill-health is partly due to other causes than poverty: but this is the chief cause.[8]

A fundamental concern about the corrigibility of the poor was central, however, to the eugenics movement (Greek for "good origins") in the early 20th century. Eugenicists, a group that included prominent figures like Alexander Graham Bell, Winston Churchill, John Maynard Keynes, and Woodrow Wilson, believed that governments should, as a national strategic imperative, take action to improve the genetic stock of their populations. While the early focus of the movement was on selective breeding, eugenicists also encouraged exclusion or sterilization of groups and individuals they considered racially or genetically unfit.

In fact, in 1927 the movement obtained a U.S. Supreme Court ruling in *Buck v. Bell* that the state of Virginia had the authority to forcibly sterilize those residents it deemed genetically defective. In a majority opinion upholding the state's decision to sterilize Carrie Buck, an eighteen-year-old deemed to have a mental age of nine who had allegedly proven "incorrigible" in school and had given birth to an illegitimate child, associate justice Oliver Wendell Holmes writes:

It is better for all the world if, instead of waiting to execute degenerate offspring for crime or to let them starve for their imbecility, society can prevent those who are manifestly unfit from continuing their kind ... Three generations of imbeciles are enough.[9]

Remarkably, though the Virginia statute was repealed in 1974, the court's ruling in the case has never been overturned.

A third expression of this view is Richard Herrnstein and Charles Murray's 1994 book, *The Bell Curve*, which presents statistical correlations between intelligence and a range of social phenomena, including poverty, crime, citizenship, and parenting, while controlling for other factors. Most controversially, the book speaks at length about the purported racial and ethnic variations in intelligence as reported on intelligence tests. The authors conclude, "It seems highly likely to us that both genes and the environment have something to do with racial differences [in intelligence]." As to the relative importance of the two factors, "the evidence does not yet justify an estimate."[10]

I embarked on this exploration with the goal of finding what is valid in each of these explanations of poverty. I now need to qualify that aspiration with respect to the genetic explanations presented above. Members of society have always hotly contested the science behind these explanations. For example, the eugenicists consistently failed to define in scientific terms the groups they considered deficient, and the movement's leaders ultimately distanced themselves from the research they themselves had funded.[11]

Regarding Herrnstein and Murray's work, some have claimed that intelligence tests are biased against non-whites and low-income people, while others have called into question the validity of the twin and adoption studies at the center of research on questions of "nature versus nurture."[12] Recent research on the brain also suggests that stress can reduce cognitive ability as indicated by an intelligence test,[13] as will be seen later in this chapter.

Further, much of the enthusiasm for the explanatory value

of genetics (e.g., finding genes for certain diseases) that existed in the late 1990s when the authors wrote *The Bell Curve* has dissipated as scientists have found genes to be much more complex than previously thought. The field of epigenetics, for example, seeks to understand how environmental factors influence gene expression,[14] blurring the traditional distinction between "nature" and "nurture." For these reasons, I am willing to let go of any explanatory value that genetics itself may have for poverty, since – to my mind – there are so many other reasons why the poor, as well as racial and ethnic minorities that are disproportionately poor, might underperform on intelligence tests.

Another expression of the *behavioral* perspective is that the poor may have both the motivation and the talent necessary for success, but their motivation is undermined by the perverse incentives of anti-poverty programs. According to Charles Murray, co-author of *The Bell Curve*:

Traditions decay when the reality facing the new generation changes. The habit of thrift decays if there is no penalty for not saving. The work ethic decays if there is no penalty for not working.[15]

Further, Murray and others argue that the Aid to Families with Dependent Children (AFDC) program that existed in the U.S. from 1935 to 1996 tended to incentivize single-parenthood and withdrawal from the workforce.[16] In some states, a single mother could lose her benefits if she spent too much time with a man, who was then deemed a "substitute parent" responsible for providing for her children.[17] (This so-called "man in the house" rule was struck down by the U.S. Supreme Court in 1968 in *King v. Smith*.) The fact that recipients could lose their social benefits if they adopted the poverty-reducing behaviors of the "success sequence" mentioned earlier, like pursuing marriage or joining the workforce, may have led many to reject those behaviors.

In the international realm, the *behavioral* view is often applied more to countries than to individuals. As compared to people living in an industrialized economy, it is harder to imagine that a villager in a low-income country is poor primarily because of her own choices rather than due to her destitute surroundings. In poor countries, the behaviors of concern are often the dereliction and corruption of officials across all levels of government.[18]

Perverse incentives may exacerbate these behaviors, as in the case of foreign aid. Economist Dambisa Moyo argues that aid from rich countries to Africa "chokes off desperately needed investment, instils a culture of dependency, and facilitates rampant and systemic corruption, all with deleterious consequences for growth." In this respect, we may see foreign aid as a poorly designed social program on a global scale. Foreign aid "perpetuates underdevelopment, and guarantees economic failure in the poorest aid-dependent countries."[19]

This suspicion of anti-poverty initiatives is not new. In criticizing the Old Poor Law in Great Britain enacted under Elizabeth I to provide support for the poor at the parish level, 19th-century economist Thomas Malthus writes:

> It is also difficult to suppose that [the Poor Laws] have not powerfully contributed to generate that carelessness and want of frugality observable among the poor, so contrary to the disposition frequently to be remarked among petty tradesmen and small farmers.[20]

While these perverse incentives introduced by social programs may have had some negative effect, the argument that these incentives were a major cause of poverty goes too far. It suggests an earlier time when these people were not poor, a notion belied by the existence of anti-poverty programs in the first place. But as poverty scholar David Ellwood writes:

> ... although [Charles] Murray is almost certainly wrong in blaming the social welfare system for a large part of the predicament of the poor, he is almost certainly correct in stating that welfare does not reflect or reinforce our most basic values [e.g., of personal responsibility]."[21]

Haskins and Sawhill echo this point when they write that "Americans believe in opportunity ... For this reason, they are more willing to support policies that reward personal responsibility and enhance mobility than policies that unconditionally redistribute income after the fact."[22]

If poverty is a behavioral failure, then what is one to do? One option would be to actively change the behaviors of the poor by dismantling or redesigning social supports that perversely incentivize them not to adopt poverty-reducing behaviors like education, employment, and marriage.

This perspective has guided recent U.S. government initiatives on poverty from Ronald Reagan's Family Support Act (1988) that emphasized work, school, and child support; to Bill Clinton's "workfare" legislation; to George W. Bush's support for faith-based behavior change initiatives; to Donald Trump's imposition of work requirements for Medicaid beneficiaries. These efforts assume that it is the government's responsibility, or at least its prerogative, to reshape the behaviors of the poor. As Reagan administration poverty advisor Lawrence Mead writes, "Competence [of the poor to take care of themselves] cannot be the assumption of social policy, but it must be the goal."[23]

If poverty derives from genetic or cognitive inferiority, then such competence may not be achievable. People with this view may instead propose sterilizing the poor (as seen in *Buck v. Bell*), "tracking" them into social and vocational roles in which they have a greater chance of success, or treating them as wards of the state. As Herrnstein and Murray predict:

> Over the next decades, it will become broadly accepted by the cognitive elite that the people we now refer to as the underclass are in that condition through no fault of their own but because of inherent shortcomings about which little can be done.[24]

What emotions would lead one to accept a *behavioral* explanation of poverty like the ones presented above? As noted in the previous chapter, there is no one-to-one map of emotions and explanations, but it seems relevant to ask why a person would find a home in this quadrant of our framework.

This perspective sees the person experiencing poverty as an "other" – it emphasizes a separation between the observer and the observed. Some emotions associated with separation include contempt (e.g., at those who live off the efforts of others), disgust (e.g., at those unwilling to take care of themselves), fear (e.g., that the indolent will undermine important social values and threaten the way of life I value), and pride in achievement (e.g., that I was born in poverty but have made my own way out). This pride may actually be the flip side of shame (e.g., of my own roots in poverty and of loved ones who may remain there). Again, the intent here is merely to start the conversation about the emotions we bring to poverty, so that we can hopefully reach a clearer understanding of poverty by releasing each perspective's emotional charge.

The emotional benefit of the *behavioral* view is certainty. It is clear that people who adopt the prescribed behaviors have an excellent chance of escaping poverty. If only more would. In this sense, the *behavioral* view may be the most factual, but the least true, of the four quadrants. The correlation between behavior and outcomes is clear, but what about the conditions that foster those behaviors?

The emotional cost of this view is that one separates oneself from others. By seeing the poor as an "other," one ignores the deeper connection that exists among us all. As a result, the person adopting this view may inflict a moral self-injury by taking cruel positions that seem logical but that become less and less tenable on an emotional basis, even though all the data stack up.

This is because the *behavioral* view largely ignores the external factors that may foster the self-defeating behaviors of the poor. "Not all parents encourage their children to do well in school; some adults can't find steady jobs; and some men and women have difficulty finding people to marry or end up in troubled marriages through no fault of their own."[25] As a result, the vaunted "success sequence" may not be equally available to everyone. Further, society has excluded some groups from opportunities to live out this sequence because of their race, gender, disabilities, or other marginalizing factors.

To understand these factors, we must visit another quadrant.

❦

The poor do their best to escape poverty, but traps and barriers keep them where they are. So claim advocates of the *structural* explanation of poverty.

This view may be so familiar to most readers that it requires little discussion. It posits that poverty is a convergence of external disadvantages rather than an inner failing of the individual.

Social welfare researcher Mark Rank has used correlations among different forms of disadvantage to create a poverty risk calculator that will tell you the likelihood that you will experience poverty at some point within one, five, ten, or fifteen years. For example, if you are a forty-year-old married black or Hispanic man with only a high school diploma, then you have a 38.8 percent chance of experiencing poverty over the next fifteen years. But that risk drops to 18.4 percent if you have the same attributes but are white.[26]

Rank argues that "American poverty is largely the result of failings at the economic and political levels, rather than at the individual level."[27] Further, his work seeks to demonstrate that many more Americans will experience poverty at some point in their lives than we might expect, making poverty *everyone's* problem rather than *someone else's* problem. However, Rank's work also demonstrates how significantly the concept of disadvantage is correlated within specific groups, among them racial and ethnic minorities.

A 2016 study by the Brookings Institution finds a significant level of correlation among five types of disadvantage: low household income, limited education, no health insurance, living in a low-income area, and unemployment. The study notes, however, that "most blacks and Hispanics are disadvantaged on at least one dimension; most whites are not." Further:

> Most whites who are disadvantaged on one
> dimension are not disadvantaged on any oth-
> ers. By contrast, most African-Americans and
> Hispanics who are disadvantaged on one dimen-
> sion are also disadvantaged on at least one more.
> Multidimensional poverty, then, is clearly much
> more common among blacks and Hispanics.[28]

Both Rank's work and the Brookings study point to race as a key barrier perpetuating poverty. This barrier has an important historical component since many past policies inhibited the creation of cross-generational wealth within certain minority populations.

For example, the Federal Housing Administration (FHA) created as part of President Franklin D. Roosevelt's "New Deal" provided guidance to U.S. mortgage lenders on where they should offer their best loans, publishing maps that color-coded neighborhoods based on their proposed viability. Neighborhoods were downgraded if they had an "undesirable population or infiltration of it," implicitly defined in racial terms.[29] The result of this so-called "redlining" was that certain groups – in particular, African-Americans – were denied opportunities for homeownership and family wealth accumulation that were available to whites.

Development economist and Nobel laureate Amartya Sen provides a prominent theory for the *structural* view. Sen defines "functionings" as "the various things a person may value doing or being," such as being well nourished and healthy or "being able to take part in the life of the community." He defines poverty, then, as a lack of "capabilities," which are "the alternative combinations of functionings that are feasible for her to achieve."[30]

This "capabilities" approach expands efforts to reduce poverty from simply increasing a country's gross national product to enhancing a wide range of personal, economic, social, and political freedoms, which proponents see both as the ends of global development and as its principal means. The UN's Human Development Index[31] and Multidimensional Poverty Index[32] reflect Sen's more expansive view.

Political philosophers Jonathan Wolff and Avner de-Shalit expand upon Sen's "capabilities" approach to describe "genuine opportunities for secure functionings," which essentially means the possibility, along multiple pathways, to realize one's potential. They use "secure" to note the difference between having such an opportunity now but not knowing how long it will last (e.g., working as a day laborer), and having an opportunity indefinitely (e.g., having a long-term employment contract). The former introduces an uncertainty that must be included in any calculation of one's aggregate disadvantage.

But what about personal responsibility, which was so central to the *behavioral* view presented earlier? Sen is relatively sanguine on this point, noting that "the people have to be seen, in this perspective, as being actively involved – given the opportunity – in shaping their own destiny."[33]

Wolff and de-Shalit, on the other hand, do not take this active involvement for granted. They argue that the individual retains responsibility for his or her own choices, and they replace "capabilities" with the term "genuine opportunity" to capture the notion that the costs associated with executing that responsibility must be reasonable. Further, "someone has a genuine opportunity for achieving a functioning ... when it is reasonable to expect him or her to take steps to achieve that functioning."[34]

But in some respects, Wolff and de-Shalit absolve the individual of responsibility in ways that would shock those holding the *behavioral* view. In one scenario, they argue that a single mother who turns down a job should continue to receive government support, since "if she were to take the job it would put several of the functionings ... at risk," including "emotional well-being, her ability to care for [her children], and possibly her health and control over the environment."[35] Further, the disadvantaged person who:

> ... might have no option but tax evasion, buying goods he knows are stolen, claiming benefits while working, and the like ... might hate what he has to do both because of the risks and because it makes him an outsider ... [A] society that is constructed in a way that in effect forces some people to break the law in order to lead a materially decent life is especially incompetent or unjust.[36]

The notion that the poor have "no option" or are "forced to break the law" suggests a stark context in which the poor have little or no room to exert personal responsibility for their lives.

Rank, Sen, and Wolff and de-Shalit frame poverty as distinct disadvantages that cannot be substituted for one another, and that often concentrate in certain populations. But what if the disadvantages reinforce one another? Then poverty becomes not just a burden but a trap.

For example, being sick can prevent you from increasing

your income (by making it more difficult for you to hold a steady job) *and* having low income may prevent you from getting healthy (because you cannot afford healthcare). Similarly, if you have no job, you cannot afford childcare, but without childcare, you have no time to look for a job.

Development economist Jeffrey Sachs describes the "poverty trap" at a macroeconomic level. He notes that there is a "ladder of development" along which a country improves its incomes, life expectancy, educational outcomes, and other dimensions while transitioning its economy from subsistence farming to light manufacturing to high-tech industries.

While most countries are on this ladder and climbing, about one-sixth of the world's population lives in countries that are not even on the ladder. As Sachs writes:

> They are trapped by disease, physical isolation, climate stress, environmental degradation, and by extreme poverty itself. Even though life-saving solutions exist to increase their chances for survival ... these families and their governments simply lack the financial means to make these crucial investments.[37]

To Sachs, the purpose of economic development is to help the poorest countries gain a foothold on the ladder, reaching what economists call a "critical threshold,"[38] since "when countries get their foot on the ladder of development, they are generally able to continue the upward climb."[39]

For Sachs, one key aspect of the poverty trap is low food productivity. Similarly, John Kenneth Galbraith describes the "equilibrium of poverty" in which increases in agricultural output allow more people not to starve, which then brings the output *per person* back to its original level. Galbraith concludes that one of the best ways for a country to break out of this equilibrium is to have large numbers of its people emigrate, since this increases the agricultural output per person.[40]

One variant of the *structural* view focuses almost exclusively on institutions, which can "forge the success or failure of nations."[41] To be successful, according to Daron Acemoglu and James Robinson, a country must have "inclusive institutions" that provide a level playing field (e.g., secure private property, rule of law, provision of public services) rather than "extractive institutions" that direct wealth toward a powerful elite.[42] Leaders are at fault when this is not the case: "Poor countries are poor because those who have power make choices that create poverty."[43]

If poverty is a structural problem, then what is one to do? One answer could be to advocate for structural reform, as in the U.S. civil rights movement of the 1960s or the current gender pay equity movement, to remove barriers that prevent poor people from obtaining the full benefit of their good efforts. One might also promote a major overhaul of the economic system, as in the Occupy movement or in protests of World Trade Organization (WTO) meetings.

Another option is to make the initial investments deemed necessary to free people and countries from the "poverty trap." For an individual, this may mean providing a resource that can be used to increase the person's income, like a farm animal from global NGO Heifer International or low-cost treadle pumps to provide irrigation for smallholder farmers.[44] For a country, this may mean helping it get on Sachs's "ladder of development" by forgiving the large-scale debt that prevents it from investing in the "inclusive institutions" called for by Acemoglu and Robinson.

The predominant emotion leading people to a *structural* explanation of poverty is anger. Wolff and de-Shalit express this anger after describing a young woman in Israel named Leah who had been thrice married, twice abandoned, and now has an unemployed husband and a child to support. They write:

> What do we feel when we read about cases like this? Many people will feel angry or frustrated. How dare these men play with Leah's life in this way? How can we tolerate social structures that force women into such dependent and confined lives?[45]

The phrase, "How can we tolerate?" points to a gross injustice that must be made right. The phrase, "How dare these men?" suggests a desire to punish or shame. Similarly, the same authors write that "the state of the least advantaged is a mark of shame and speaks poorly of Western societies."[46]

Some may come to this explanation through guilt. If people have achieved outcomes in life that they cannot honestly describe as justly deserved, then they may ask: Did I do something unfair, or is the system itself unfair? Obviously, the latter is the more palatable answer. Thus, some of the anger directed toward the system may substitute for the guilt that the unjustly successful prefer not to feel.

Guilt may also come from a sense of shared cultural identity with those who subjugated, colonized, or enslaved other peoples. Anger expressed at the long-term consequences of such actions distinguishes us from those at fault and may serve as a form of repentance for the transgressions of one's forebears.

The emotional benefit of this view is righteousness, a form of emotional or moral certainty. The person adopting this view may think, "The world may be unfair, but at least I'm doing something about it." The problem then becomes the other people who are not. As Wolff and de-Shalit write, a person's "disadvantage may well have been created by others, or, if not, is at least tolerated by them."[47]

The emotional cost of this view is an exhausting level of vigilance. One must always be alert to injustice lest one should inadvertently merge into the silent masses who are doing nothing. While people taking this view may pay disproportionate attention to the injustice inflicted upon people like themselves, at least philosophically they have made a commitment to resist injustice in all its forms.

Although the *structural* view has gained ground in recent years in intellectual circles (though less so in policy circles in the U.S.), its relative inattention to the behaviors by which the poor often work against their own interests strikes some as going too far, even – in the case of Wolff and de-Shalit – ostensibly justifying criminality. Such behaviors require greater explanation than simply, "The system made me do it."

But how can we explain these behaviors without assuming that the poor are fundamentally derelict, incompetent, or corrupted? To answer this question, we must visit another quadrant.

∽

Poor people perpetuate their own poverty through the bad decisions they make, but these decisions make sense given the absurd context in which they live. So claim adherents of the *contextual* explanation of poverty. But how could the counterproductive decisions of the poor, like not working or not seeking employable skills, ever *make sense*?

Philosopher Charles Karelis suggests that the behavior of the poor makes sense not because it fits a model of rational behavior developed by economists, but because that model does not apply to the poor. Karelis points to the law of marginal utility, which states that each additional unit of a good (e.g., a product or service) provides the consumer with less utility (e.g., pleasure, satisfaction) than the previous unit. In plain language, you will enjoy your first ice cream sundae more than you will your fourth or fifth.

Karelis argues that this law flips upside-down in the case of the poor. If you have 100 bee stings, then taking care of one bee sting will not have much impact on your overall comfort. So why bother? Similarly, it is rational for the poor not to take action to solve their problems, since they would inevitably still have many more problems than they could solve.[48]

Sometimes it may make sense for the poor to just give up; this variant of the *contextual* view relies on "temporal uncertainty." If you are waiting for a train but do not know what time it will arrive, then you have to decide whether or not to keep waiting. In the absence of cues that tell you the train is coming soon, such as a monitor along the platform, it may be rational – rather than a lack of self-control, as it may seem – to get in a taxi, start walking, or just go home.[49]

Along the same lines, behavioral economists Abhijit Banerjee and Esther Duflo note that the poor "often behave as if they think that any change that is significant enough to be worth sacrificing for will simply take too long. This could explain why they focus on the here and now, on living their lives as pleasantly as possible, [spending their money on] celebrating [rather than on basic necessities] when occasion demands it."[50]

A current popular view contends that the stresses inherent in the experience of poverty lead the poor to make decisions that ultimately work against them. However, this response is perfectly natural, and we could expect it of *anyone* who finds himself or herself in poverty. According to the World Bank's 2015 World Development Report:

> Poverty is not simply a shortfall of money. The constant, day-to-day hard choices associated with poverty in effect "tax" an individual's psychological and social resources ... and can lead to economic decisions that perpetuate poverty.[51]

For example, the poor experience a "bandwidth tax" that limits their cognitive capacity and executive function simply as a consequence of the scarcity they face. After all, it is hard to concentrate on checking your children's homework or looking for a higher-paying job if you are struggling to put food on the table.

In studies, the decrement in cognitive capacity associated with the experience of scarcity is as high as thirteen to fourteen IQ points. And while such reductions can occur with any kind of scarcity (e.g., a professional working to meet a tight deadline), they play a disproportionate role in the lives of the poor, since unlike other forms of scarcity, "one cannot take a vacation from poverty."[52]

In *Scarcity*, Mullainathan and Shafir describe the "bandwidth tax" and other stress effects scarcity can bring. Poor people may "tunnel," which means that they focus single-mindedly on the immediate situation and ignore important issues outside that "tunnel." They may "borrow" from the future to address today's crisis, for example, by taking out a high-interest "payday loan." Mullainathan and Shafir equate this with a busy professional's postponing typing up notes from a meeting, only to need more time to decipher those notes later once the memory of the meeting has dissipated. Poor people also face a "lack of slack," which means essentially that they have much less room for error or adjustment than do people with greater resources.[53]

Similarly, the poor may experience "decision fatigue," in which the high stakes of every financial decision they make (e.g., can I afford milk this week, or should I wait until my next paycheck?) exhausts the decision-making apparatus in their brains. At some point, they begin to select the default options or take no action at all, even if those outcomes are not in their best interest.[54]

To reduce this effect, scientists who study "decision fatigue" encourage people to automate as many decisions as possible so that they can focus their mental energy on decisions that require their direct involvement. Of course, the poor have fewer decisions that can be automated. First, they have much less slack in their resources, and second, tools for automating decision-making may be less common where they live. As a result, poverty itself can lead to decisions that tend to keep a person poor.

If poverty is a contextual problem, then what is one to do? The most obvious answer is to eliminate the scarcity. Rutger Bregman suggests doing this through a basic guaranteed income, which would ensure that everyone in a society has enough income to secure the basic necessities.[55] In the U.S., this idea was introduced during the Nixon Administration as the Family Assistance Plan (FAP), which would have ensured a minimum income while requiring everyone to work except for mothers of small children.[56] Mounting opposition on the left and right prevented passage of the law, but several pilots of basic guaranteed income are currently underway in the U.S., as in Europe,[57] and public support for the idea is increasing.[58]

Another answer may be to protect the poor from their own behaviors under stress. For example, the SEED program (Save, Earn, Enjoy Deposits), launched in 2002 by the Green Bank of Caraga in the Philippines, offers savings accounts to which clients can restrict their own access either by date (like a certificate of deposit) or by minimum balance. After one year, the program's first set of clients saved over 300 percent more than they would have without the accounts.[59]

Another approach would be to reward poor people – through conditional cash transfers (CCTs) – for behaviors that will tend to help them escape poverty. In Brazil, for example, the government's Bolsa Família program pays parents to keep their children in school and take them to routine medical check-ups.[60]

The emotions related to the *contextual* explanation are a little more difficult to discern, but let us try. There is a clear desire to give the poor the benefit of the doubt and to see the world from their point of view. Banerjee and Duflo write that "the natural place to start to unravel the mystery [of the poor's behavior] is to assume that the poor must know what they are doing."[61] By arguing that "poverty – the scarcity mindset – causes failure,"[62] Mullainathan and Shafir explicitly seek to create an "empathy bridge" that allows people facing *any* form of scarcity, such as a busy professional, to relate to those living in poverty: "Under these conditions [of scarcity], we all would have (and have!) failed."[63]

But empathy is less an emotion than it is an intention to connect to the emotions experienced by others. Perhaps adherents of this view seek to connect to the shame (the "other"-ness) felt by the poor, and by validating the presumed rationality of the poor they produce a feeling of comfort, both for themselves and vicariously for the poor. The poor can feel at ease knowing that they are not so different after all, and the non-poor can feel at ease with them.

Similarly, this view may reflect feelings of frustration that after so many years, poverty still exists. The *contextual* view is a simple solution to a problem that has confronted humans for a long time. The poor, proponents argue, are no different from the rich. They just need help reducing their stress so that they can bring their best decision-making to bear on the problems of their lives.

The emotional benefit of this view is a sense of relief – the reasoned conclusion that poverty may not be so difficult to solve after all, that "a sense of possibility and a little bit of well-targeted help (a piece of information, a little nudge) can sometimes have surprisingly large effects."[64] We just need to ensure a basic income, enroll the poor in programs that automate their decision-making, and incentivize short-term behaviors with long-term payoffs.

The emotional cost of this view is avoidance of the deeper psychological issues that may undermine the presumption that the poor are as rational as everyone else. By assuming the poor's rationality *a priori*, this view allows one to focus attention on psychological and theoretical studies that may not even include the poor, though the findings are applied to the poor after the fact. This explanation shines a spotlight on one aspect of poverty and then finds solace in not seeing anything in the darkness that escapes it.

But are the poor rational? How far can the argument go that we would all make similarly bad decisions under the stresses of poverty? Many readers may wonder if – even under great stress – they would need to be paid to enroll their children in school, or if they would, like mothers described by Banerjee and Duflo,[65] refuse to deworm their children for the cost of a few cents. Might Ben Carson have been on to something when he spoke of a "poverty mindset"?

For that, we must move on to the last of our four quadrants.

∽◎

Poverty results from a coherent set of attitudes and behaviors that tend to keep people poor. This is the view of those who embrace the *cultural* explanation of poverty.

For centuries, observers have consistently noted the same behaviors among the poor, including a short-term orientation, a fatalism regarding the future, and an attitude of opportunistic hedonism. For example, 19th-century economist Thomas Malthus writes:

> The labouring poor, to use a vulgar expression, seem always to live from hand to mouth. Their present wants employ their whole attention, and they seldom think of the future.[66]

Karl Marx described a "lumpenproletariat" that:

> ... in all towns forms a mass quite distinct from the more respectable industrial proletariat. It is a recruiting ground for thieves and criminals

of all sorts, living off the garbage of society ...
vagabonds, *gens sans feu et sans aveu*, varying according to the cultural level of their particular
nation.[67]

The attitudes and behaviors cited here resemble those from
the *behavioral* view, but they are attributed not to individual inadequacy or dereliction but rather to the shared norms of an
entire community. They constitute a coherent set of attitudes
and behaviors that tend to keep the community poor.

Anthropologist Oscar Lewis coined the term "culture of
poverty" in the 1950s to describe what he viewed as:

... a culture in the traditional anthropological
sense in that it provides human beings with a
design for living, with a ready-made set of solutions for human problems, and so serves a significant adaptive function.[68]

While many observers describe the lives of the poor as unstable
and disorderly, Lewis reports being struck by "the inexorable
repetitiousness and the iron entrenchment of their lifeways."[69]

According to Lewis, the "culture of poverty" has the following features. The poor in general do not engage with social
and political institutions, of which they are often suspicious or
fearful. Within their own communities, they lack a clear social
structure that reaches across the boundaries of individual families, except perhaps for gangs, which Lewis considered "a con-
siderable advance" in organization. Families have low rates of
consensual marriage and high rates of female-headed households, and parents do little to protect childhood as a time for

growth and development. As individuals, the poor suffer from weak ego structures, a strong present orientation, a reduced ability to defer gratification, and a belief in male superiority. Further, they embrace provincial attitudes that ignore events happening elsewhere.[70]

Michael Harrington popularized Lewis's "culture of poverty" in his 1962 surprise bestseller, *The Other America*. While much of Harrington's book addresses macroeconomic shifts that had both challenged the poor and rendered them invisible (and are more consistent with the *structural* explanation described earlier), it also characterizes the psychology of poverty.

Harrington describes the "lower social economic status individual" as "rigid, suspicious and [having] a fatalistic outlook on life. They do not plan ahead, … are prone to depression, have feelings of futility, lack of belongingness, friendliness, and a lack of trust in others."[71] Harrington adds that the poor tend to act out, to be less inhibited, and to be violent.

One of the most famous – and infamous – publications associated with this view is *The Negro Family: A Case for National Action* (1965), also called the "Moynihan Report" as it was authored by assistant secretary of labor, and later U.S. senator, Daniel Patrick Moynihan. In the report, Moynihan argues that despite the recent Civil Rights Act of 1964, African-Americans would continue to suffer from the residual effects of slavery and segregation unless the nation endeavored to heal the "tangle of pathology" within the African-American family.

The events surrounding the release of the Moynihan Report were so traumatic for liberals that the report remains a lightning rod even a half-century later. We will explore this in the next chapter. Notably, Moynihan's attribution of this "tangle of pathology" to African-American culture itself is inconsistent with

Lewis's premise that the "culture of poverty" transcends national, racial, ethnic, and urban-rural differences, and that traits often attributed to African-Americans were present even in poor populations with no experience of racial discrimination.[72]

In the late 1960s and 1970s, liberals generally turned away from the "culture of poverty" construct they had created. William Julius Wilson later criticized his liberal colleagues for refusing to discuss the behaviors of the poor for fear of being attacked as Moynihan had been.[73] As liberals backed away, however, conservatives in the U.S. took up the construct, embellished it with racialized images like the "welfare queen" of the black ghetto, and used it to alter social programs in ways that liberals found objectionable, such as reducing eligibility or attaching work requirements.

Edward Banfield supported such reforms. A political scientist and an advisor to Presidents Nixon, Ford, and Reagan, Banfield believed the government could do little to shape class culture, which he viewed as a primary driver of socioeconomic outcomes. Banfield characterizes class culture in terms of one's "psychological orientation toward the future,"[74] and describes a "lower-class individual" as someone who "lives from moment to moment ... [and sees the future as] fixed, fated, beyond his control. Impulse governs his behavior ... [He] has a feeble, attenuated sense of self ... he is suspicious and hostile, aggressive yet dependent."[75]

Lewis describes the "culture of poverty" fundamentally as an adaptation to the condition of poverty and to the feelings of hopelessness that result. John Kenneth Galbraith echoes this view when he discusses the poor's "accommodation" to poverty.[76] Harrington defends this adaptation, noting that:

... the smug theorist of the middle class would probably deplore [the immediate gratification of the poor] as showing a lack of traditional American virtues. Actually, it is the logical and natural pattern of behavior for one living in a part of American life without a future."[77]

Galbraith makes a similar comment that "the one thing worse than accepting the equilibrium and culture of poverty was to live in hopeless conflict with it."[78]

More recently, Ruby Payne has revived the *cultural* view of poverty for an audience of educators who teach poor children. Payne's cognitive framing of poverty describes the "hidden rules" that exist for each social class:

Hidden rules are about the salient, unspoken understandings that cue the members of the group that a given individual does or does not fit ... Generally, in order to successfully move from one class to the next, it is important to have a spouse or mentor from the class to which you wish to move to model and teach you the hidden rules.[79]

The hidden rules of the poor that Payne identifies echo the earlier descriptions of the "culture of poverty" from Lewis, Harrington, and Banfield. (Of course, she draws upon this research.) The poor use money disproportionately for entertainment, which provides a respite from the struggle of poverty. Families tend to be matriarchal and "the key issue for males is to be a 'man,' ... to work hard physically – and be a lover and a fighter."[80] Perhaps most significantly, the poor person "sees [the] world in terms of [his or her own] local setting," and "believes in fate; [he or she] cannot do much to mitigate chance."[81]

Recent research on parenting styles offers another variant of the *cultural* view. Sociologist Annette Lareau conducted a longitudinal qualitative study of twelve families across four classes (rich, middle class, working class, and poor). She concludes that parents apply different "cultural logics" to the task of raising children.

Rich and middle-class parents undertake what Lareau calls "concerted cultivation" in which "discussions between parents and children" as well as "organized activities, established and controlled by mothers and fathers," foster:

> a robust sense of entitlement ... This sense of entitlement plays an especially important role in institutional settings, where middle-class children learn to question adults and address them as relative equals.[82]

By contrast, working-class and poor parents do not elicit "their children's feelings, opinions, and thoughts," they "see a clear boundary between adults and children," and they "tend to use directives: they tell their children what to do rather than persuading them with reasoning." Their children "have more control over the character of their leisure activities" and "are free to go out and play with friends and relatives who typically live close by." Lareau calls this parenting style the "accomplishment of natural growth."[83]

Unlike Lewis, Lareau sees nothing intrinsically wrong with either parenting style. For example, while rich and middle-class children learn how to shake hands with adults and look them in the eye, working-class and poor children learn how to occupy themselves for long stretches of time without adult attention.

To Lareau, the problem arises when working-class and poor children interact with social institutions such as schools. Because the cultural logic of their homes – what Payne would call the "hidden rules" – is out of sync with the rich and middle-class logic promoted and adopted by social institutions, these less-advantaged children develop a sense not of entitlement but of "distance, distrust, and constraint."[84]

Lareau asserts that the parenting style of working-class and poor parents results from the economic pressures they face. While they "want the best" for their children, "formidable economic constraints" make parenting more of a challenge than it is for wealthier parents.[85] Further, these parents may lack the knowledge they need (e.g., how to complete a college application) to help their children succeed. Lareau concludes that much of the difference in parenting styles may derive from structural factors.

Lewis clearly sees it differently. As he writes, "The family in the culture of poverty does not cherish childhood as a specially prolonged and protected stage in the life cycle."[86] The issue is not economic constraints but rather the norms and values that parents in some poor communities bring to the task of parenting. If he is right, then the choices of working-class and poor parents may, to some extent, reflect apathy and neglect rather than simply high stress and a lack of middle-class know-how.

If poverty is a *cultural* failure, then what is one to do? Payne advises teachers to teach poor children the "hidden rules" of middle-class life, not as the "right" answer but as the most likely way for them to enter the middle class. Government efforts like Head Start have tried to offset the negative impacts of the "culture of poverty" earlier in the life course, in part by providing a substitute for learning that may not occur in the home. Other efforts include programs to instill in the poor the values and habits of cleanliness, order, and organized living.

What emotions would lead one to this explanation of poverty? To the extent that the *cultural* view is simply the *behavioral* view writ across an entire community, the emotions undergirding it may be the same: fear, contempt, and disgust. This may be especially true of the "culture of poverty" in its racialized form. For those who have escaped poverty, this view may coincide with pride at having shed the self-destructive mindset into which they were born, with sadness that it was their lot to begin with, or with grief over what might have been, had they been born otherwise. This may be true of Moynihan, whose fatherless childhood in the Hell's Kitchen neighborhood of New York City likely mirrored much of what he described in his eponymous report.

But presumably left-leaning thinkers like Lewis and Harrington feel differently. As his *New York Times* obituary notes, Lewis "had an enormous compassion for the people whose ways he recorded."[87] Like those taking the *contextual* view, he too wanted to give the poor the benefit of the doubt, and thus characterized the poor's behavior not as individual dereliction but as an effective and coherent adaptation to their circumstances. As Lewis writes:

> The confusion [between conceptions of the poor as alternatively blessed or mean] results also from the tendency to focus study and attention on the personality of the individual victim of

poverty rather than on the slum community and family and from the consequent failure to distinguish between [economic] poverty and what I have called the culture of poverty.[88]

Perhaps the early adherents of the "culture of poverty" view felt the same excitement exhibited by behavioral economists and brain scientists embracing the *contextual* view today, except that their new technology for understanding the poor was not brain scans and randomized controlled trials, but rather an anthropological method for living with the poor and observing them firsthand, as Lewis had done. Whereas the *contextual* view assumes the rationality of the poor, the *cultural* view assumes that the poor behave irrationally, but coherently and justifiably so.

The emotional benefits of this view are security and absolution. Attitudes and behaviors that on the individual level could be quite threatening are attributed to something larger, a broader cultural adaptation to difficult circumstances. Further, the scale of the problem puts it beyond anything one person alone could do.

The emotional cost of this view is despair. Given the extensive suffering in the world, it is sad to think that we humans bring much of it upon ourselves. We establish our mindsets early in life, and they often allow for us only what we already find familiar. Thus, hidden rules of behavior and unconscious beliefs constrain what might otherwise be possible for our futures.

This chapter has presented four contrasting explanations of poverty that are based on the different assumptions we each might bring to the issue. All these perspectives have some validity, and the broader emotional and cognitive space that would allow us to think and feel differently about poverty would allow each perspective to be true in its own way.

But one of these four perspectives has been particularly maligned in recent decades by the political left, such that it requires rehabilitation before we can craft a new way of thinking about poverty that retains the best aspects of all four. This is the *cultural* perspective just presented above. This is where we now turn our attention.

CHAPTER THREE

Rehabilitating the "Culture of Poverty"

"While people may be quite aware of their early life challenges,
they still may be seriously unaware of how their choices in people,
environments, decisions, behaviors, and attitudes are connected to those
experiences and how those choices are the major factor in their current
predicaments and unhappiness."

Dr. Laura Schlessinger

Up to this point, I have spoken equally of all four explanations of poverty, highlighting the emotional costs and
benefits of each. Now, however, I want to focus specifically on
the views of my colleagues who place themselves in the *structural* quadrant of our framework. This is the perspective I come
across most frequently in my consulting and teaching work, so
in my own sphere, I have come to see this view as the default.

In my experience, people holding this view often have a
visceral resistance to any suggestion that the poor contribute to
their own poverty, as implied by the "culture of poverty" construct discussed at the end of the previous chapter. I believe this
resistance is unwarranted, or at least disproportionate, and that
relaxing it would foster a more effective discussion of poverty.
On a practical level, allowing room for the agency of the poor

may improve the likelihood of enacting the systemic reforms that those taking the *structural* view would like to see.

The "culture of poverty" construct was racialized in the U.S. for political advantage from the 1960s onward, particularly as political leaders focused their attention on African-American poverty in the inner city. For this reason, in the imagination of the political left, the "culture of poverty" construct is closely associated with racism, with the mass incarceration of black men, and with reductions in social assistance to single black mothers. As Afro-American history professor Touré Reed provocatively writes, "All roads named culture of poverty lead to mass incarceration."[1]

It is critical, then, to acknowledge the destructive role this concept has played with respect to race and to distinguish the racialized use of the term "culture of poverty" from what I intend here, though I know this will be difficult for many readers to do. I am using Lewis's original construct, which describes behaviors observed in poor populations regardless of race, ethnicity, or historical experience of slavery or discrimination. Lewis conducted the fieldwork that gave rise to this construct in India, Mexico, and Puerto Rico. He was clear in his writing that many traits often attributed to African-Americans were equally observable in poor populations elsewhere.

This distinction between the original and the subsequently racialized version of the construct is timely. In the U.S., the ongoing opioid epidemic and the election of Donald Trump to the presidency are bringing more attention to poor white communities that fit the "culture of poverty" description. As J.D. Vance notes:

Appalachian whites suffer from many of the

same social ills as working-class blacks: broken families, substance abuse, poor health, and high poverty.[2]

So, I ask those readers who are particularly resistant to the construct due to its use in racial politics in the U.S. to at least entertain the notion that it may refer to something that transcends race, ethnicity, and nationality as the basis for the discussion that follows.

First, we must ask: Do the poor behave differently from the non-poor? There seems to be a good deal of consensus that they do, even across all four of the quadrants discussed in the previous chapter.

In the *behavioral* quadrant, Haskins and Sawhill show that households that follow the "success sequence" of finishing high school, working in a job, and getting married before having children have only a 2 percent chance of living in poverty. Whatever the cause, the chronically poor clearly deviate from these norms.

In the *cultural* quadrant, Lewis and others describe the poor as socially disengaged, provincially minded, present-focused, and impulsive. More sympathetically than those taking the *behavioral* view, they characterize these behaviors as a coherent way of life that "is also something positive and provides some rewards without which the poor could hardly carry on."[3]

Within the *contextual* view, Mullainathan and Shafir note that "the poor fall short in many ways" and that "when you look at the data, these factors [of access and cost and skills] alone cannot explain the failures ... at the core there is a problem of behavior."[4] Banerjee and Duflo conclude that the poor lack the "mental space" to take a longer view of their lives and that, "Perhaps [the] idea that there is a future is what makes the difference between the poor and the middle class."[5]

Even proponents of the *structural* view acknowledge these behaviors. Susan Greenbaum, while critiquing the "culture of poverty" construct, writes of "families with dad in jail and mom a hopeless addict, where older kids are likely to end up on the streets ... such families and teens do exist in too large numbers in Tampa and most other cities."[6]

"Culture of poverty" critic William Ryan recognizes the behavioral differences of the poor, but attributes them to poverty itself:

> What some are accustomed to thinking of as the enduring debilitating characteristics of the poor – such as apathy, fatalism, depression, and pessimism – are actually the straightforward manifestations of the dynamics arising from lack of power. Man powerless is not fully man.[7]

Taking a similar line, Brazilian educationalist Paulo Freire writes that:

> Fatalism in the guise of docility ... almost always is related to the power of destiny or fate or fortune – inevitable forces – or to a distorted view of God. Under the sway of magic and myth, the oppressed (especially the peasants, who are almost submerged in nature) see their suffering, the fruit of exploitation, as the will of God – as if God were the creator of this "organized disorder."

But to Freire, this fatalism "is the fruit of an historical and sociological situation, not an essential characteristic of a people's behavior."[8]

It seems that the disagreement among these views is not so much in terms of the behaviors observed, but in terms of the meaning ascribed to those behaviors.

∞

In the previous chapter, I suggested that the primary emotion underlying the *structural* explanation of poverty is anger. With this in mind, visceral resistance to the notion that the poor contribute to their own poverty makes sense. Anger is the emotion we feel when we encounter what we assess to be an injustice. If we view poverty as an injustice committed against the poor, then our natural response will be to eliminate the injustice and to punish those responsible.

Acknowledging the agency of the poor undermines the legitimacy of that punishment, since those to be punished are not completely to blame. They have the poor as their accomplices.

Further, it makes it more difficult to muster the political support for structural changes to correct the injustice. As Eleanor Burke Leacock writes, reference to the "culture of poverty" in the 1960s "served to mask the crucial issue of social and economic justice that our society must face."[9] Monique Redeaux criticizes "culture of poverty" proponents for failing to "indict the corrupt system responsible for making and keeping people poor."[10]

William Ryan suggests that those who speak of a "culture of poverty" are guilty of a hypocrisy reflecting their own inner conflicts – that "the fruits of this ideology appear to be fraught with altruism and humanitarianism, so it is hard to believe that it is principally functional to block social change."[11] The middle class want to be seen as helping, but at the same time, they are loath to reform the systems that ensure their privilege and position.

So, the visceral reaction makes sense as a manifestation of this underlying anger and desire to punish. To fully understand it, however, we need to trace its roots back to the 1960s and to the important shifts – and traumas – that occurred in the U.S. during that decade.

The confluence of dynamics in play at that point in history continues to shape the poverty conversation. In particular, these three forces have challenged the traditional poverty discourse that had existed up until that point: inclusion of more diverse perspectives on social issues, fundamental shifts in gender roles and family structure, and the rise of a youth generation eager to upend existing systems. These also set the stage for the liberal trauma of the Moynihan Report, the effects of which resonate to this day.

In the 1960s, new social movements were bringing new voices – e.g., African-Americans, women, youth – into the public discourse. This was true internationally as well with the independence of former colonies of European powers, particularly in Africa. Such groups at long last could openly express their long-standing anger over past grievances, or in some cases, they were recognizing for the first time how poorly they had been treated. In the adage often attributed to Gloria Steinem, "The truth will set you free, but first it will piss you off." Broader participation changed how we discussed social issues and focused attention on the structural factors that allowed many of the social problems to persist.

A new generation – the so-called Baby Boomers – was coming on to the scene in the U.S., and many of these young people decried the stale, secular systems which their (G.I. generation) grandparents had crafted and to which their (Silent generation) parents had dutifully conformed. These young people on the so-called New Left, which sought a wide range of social changes, exhorted one another, "Don't trust anyone over thirty."[12] They called into question the old ways of viewing things. They replaced the so-called "Negro problem," long studied from a distance by white politicians and academics, with a struggle for civil rights. Social norms around sex and gender began to unravel. A global movement to protect the environment began to take shape.

William Strauss and Neil Howe, who have written extensively on differences among generations and who coined generational nicknames like "Generation X" and "Millennials," note Boomers' desire to live out their innermost values and to see those values reflected in the outer world.[13] For this so-called "Me generation," settling for anything less was not an option. This is true of both the liberals of the New Left and of their ideological adversaries who drove the success of the conservative and evangelical movements, in a way doubling down on the values of the old system. The battle lines drawn between these two camps in the 1960s have shaped U.S. politics – and the domestic poverty discourse – to this day.

For the left, these forces produced a greater desire – and even a moral imperative – to fundamentally transform society if we were to continue to make progress. Rev. Dr. Martin Luther King Jr. captured this feeling when he wrote:

To accept passively an unjust system is to

cooperate with that system; thereby the oppressed become as evil as the oppressor.
Noncooperation with evil is as much a moral obligation as is cooperation with good.[14]

If the political left's general orientation since the 1960s has
been that the system is unjust and that accepting an unjust system makes one "as evil as the oppressor," then it makes sense
that the left could only see the poor as an oppressed group
whose lives are an active, daily struggle against their oppressor. Any suggestion to the contrary would undermine the left's
political logic.

Liberals had to make a choice in how they conceptualized
poverty. Either the poor needed to do better in the existing system or society needed to replace the system itself. Each course
of action implied its own intellectual conception of poverty. As
Susan Greenbaum writes:

The structure imposes disadvantages, but individuals damage themselves by making bad
choices; poverty outcomes derive from both. The
ultimate question is, which causes which? Are
broken families the dependent or independent
variable? Does marital instability result from unfair job opportunities for young black men? Or,
do female-headed households nurture children
who become unemployable? ... In terms of both
theory and policy, these questions matter.[15]

The left chose to see structural disadvantage as the cause
of behavioral failure and as the appropriate (and perhaps only)

target for reform. As William Ryan writes:

> The overwhelming majority of the poor are poor
> because they have, first: insufficient income; and
> second: no access to methods of increasing that
> income – that is, no power. They are too young,
> too old, too sick; they are bound to the task of
> caring for small children, or they are simply dis-
> criminated against. The facts are clear, and the
> solution seems rather obvious – raise their in-
> come and let their "culture," whatever it might
> be, take care of itself.[16]

For the right, behavior was primary. Lawrence Mead, a
policy advisor to President Ronald Reagan, argues that the
1960s saw a shift in poverty policy from improving the lives
of Americans who worked, to coping with the dependency
of those who did not.[17] The right had far less patience for this
group and advocated for policies to change their behavior, such
as scaling back social programs and creating new work requirements for eligibility.

Conservatives seem to have won the argument, at least for
now. Remarkably, the best-known legislative accomplishment
of President Bill Clinton, a Democrat, was the 1996 Personal
Responsibility and Work Opportunity Act that replaced long-
term benefits with transitional payments of limited duration.
Under the Trump administration two decades later, even
Medicaid may end up with work requirements in some states.

By contrast, arguably the left's most prominent legislative
achievement during this period, President Barack Obama's
Patient Protection and Affordable Care Act, or "Obamacare," as

of the time of this writing has a very uncertain future. It would seem, then, that at least for now, the system the left has decried for fifty years as unjust is relatively safe and secure.

The same period saw a significant increase in economic inequality in the U.S. Whereas the average CEO earned twenty times the salary of the average worker in 1965, by 2013 he (the average CEO is male) earned 295.9 times as much.[18] The richest one percent of Americans accounted for 39.6 percent of all U.S. wealth in 2016, up from 33.4 percent in 1962, and their share of income increased over the same period from 8.4 percent to more than one-fifth.[19]

Maybe this was not the left's fault. They may have just been on the wrong side of history, and it may be that the political winds are starting to blow in the opposite direction. After four decades of government expansion, from the New Deal to the Great Society, it makes sense that the country would want to slow down a little, or even – as conservative author William F. Buckley put it – stand athwart history and yell "stop!" The New Left wanted more radical change; the "Silent Majority" was not so sure.

But it may also be that the left's refusal to acknowledge that the poor play at least some role in creating their own situation has contributed to the right's political success over the past fifty years. This refusal has put the left's narrative on poverty at odds with the fact, according to Haskins and Sawhill, that "Americans believe in opportunity. They believe that anyone who works hard and has a certain amount of talent can get ahead."[20] David Ellwood argues that the goal of U.S. social policy should be "a system that ensures that everyone *who exercises reasonable responsibility* can make it without welfare."[21]

Each of us knows that we have choices to make in life and

that sometimes we choose well and sometimes we choose poorly. We know that in general, we face the consequences of the choices we make. Why would it be any different for the poor?

Perhaps the left has failed to produce a compelling political narrative because it has denied what all of us in our own lives know to be true. If that is true, then acknowledging the agency of the poor offers practical value for enacting structural reforms that have eluded the left for more than a generation.

That the left would deny the poor some level of control over their own lives seems even more bizarre when one considers other ideas that have gained popularity in the U.S. over the same period. Since the 1960s, a burgeoning self-help movement has spread the notion that each of us – among the non-poor at least – contributes to our own life outcomes through patterns of thought and action that we can identify and – if we choose – reprogram. While self-improvement has always been a cornerstone of middle-class values, current leaders in the self-help movement argue that one can achieve such improvement simply by changing one's thoughts.

For example, prominent coaches like Tony Robbins tell us that we can fundamentally change how we experience life by changing how we direct our thoughts. Robbins writes:

> I've taught for many years about the power of being in an "energy-rich" state: a peak state where you can accomplish anything and where your relationships are filled with passion. By contrast, when you're in an "energy-poor" state, the body feels lazy, the mind feels sluggish, and you can't do anything much but worry, get frustrated, and snap at people! ... We can't control all

the events in our lives, but we can control what those events mean to us – and thus what we feel and experience every day of our lives![22]

Some even suggest that scarcity – a key feature of the *contextual* view – is simply a mental construct, an illusion. In her book, *The Soul of Money*, NGO fundraiser and activist Lynne Twist writes:

> We each have the choice in any setting to step back and let go of the mind-set of scarcity. Once we let go of scarcity, we discover the surprising truth of sufficiency [that is, that we have enough] … I am not suggesting that there is ample water in the desert or food for the beggars in Bombay. I am saying that even in the presence of genuine scarcity of external resources, the desire and capacity for self-sufficiency are innate and enough to meet the challenges we face. It is precisely when we turn our attention to these inner resources – in fact, only when we do that – that we can begin to see more clearly the sufficiency in us and available to us, and we can begin to generate effective, sustainable responses to whatever limitations of resources confront us.[23]

In *You Are a Badass*, Jen Sincero argues that even how we speak to ourselves can shape our financial outcomes. She writes:

> When we say we want money for something, we often come from a place of "I don't have it, it

does not exist, so I need to create it." This has us focusing on, and believing in, lack, thereby lowering our frequency [that is, a spiritual kind of resonance] and attracting more lack.[24]

The ideas themselves are not new; they have simply gained more currency in recent years. Early examples of this worldview include *The Science of Getting Rich* (1910) by William Wattles, *The Master Key System* (1916) by Charles Haanel, and Napoleon Hill's 1937 classic, *Think and Grow Rich*, which begins:

Truly, 'thoughts are things,' and powerful things at that, when they are mixed with definiteness of purpose, persistence, and a BURNING DESIRE for their translation into money, or other material riches.[25]

Mainstream psychology has also begun to focus more on how our mindsets affect our abilities to learn and to succeed in life. Carol Dweck distinguishes between a "fixed mindset," in which failure is viewed as validation of one's inadequacy, and a "growth mindset," in which failure is viewed as an opportunity to learn.[26] Many schools are now discussing these two mindsets explicitly with students as a means to change the narrative inside their heads, and research suggests that even limited exposure to the concepts can bring about observable improvements in student performance.

Kelly McGonigal extols the benefits of stress, another concept central to the *contextual* view. She points to research showing that the negative health effects of stress largely disappear for those who do not believe that stress is bad for their health.

Further, she highlights the positive aspects of the body's stress response, namely that it prepares the person to respond to a challenge and it prompts them (through the release of the hormone oxytocin) to connect with others who can offer support.[27]

Similarly, research shows that even the most extreme cases of trauma can ultimately prove positive for a person's well-being. While some suffer from post-traumatic stress disorder (PTSD), others may experience post-traumatic growth (PTG), in which they "develop new understandings of themselves, the world they live in, how to relate to other people, the kind of future they might have and a better understanding of how to live life."[28] This is different from saying some people are more resilient than others; people with greater resilience may be less likely to experience post-traumatic growth since they may not be "rocked to the core" by the traumatic event.[29]

Others point to the body as an instrument for improving the outcomes we achieve. Harvard social psychologist Amy Cuddy writes that by adopting "power poses" (e.g., standing with our arms stretched into the air) that make us feel strong and confident before difficult situations, we can produce a fundamental shift in what we attain in our lives.[30] We get that job. We attract a mate. We make more money. In colloquial terms, we can "fake it to make it."

The prevailing view seems to be that our mindsets play a key role in shaping our life outcomes. Our circumstances are not just the result of all the external factors acting upon us – of all the disadvantages Mark Rank uses to predict our future chances of being poor. We participate in the creation of our circumstances through what we think, feel, and do. Isn't this what Ben Carson was saying?

Contrast this message, then, with these words from "culture of poverty" critic William Ryan:

In real life, style tends to follow close on money, and money tends to be magnetized and attracted to power. Those who try to persuade us that the process can be reversed, that a change in style of life can lead backward to increased wealth and greater power, are preaching nonsense. To promise that improved table manners can produce a salary increase; that more elegant taste in clothes will lead to the acquisition of stock in IBM, that an expanded vocabulary will automatically generate an enlargement of community influence – these are pernicious as well as foolish.[31]

No one would argue that changing such behaviors would "automatically" improve one's financial situation. As the Fox News panelist said in Chapter 1, "You cannot blink yourself out of poverty." But are we really to believe that for the poor (unlike for the rest of us), changing one's behavior has *no* effect even over a longer period of time? If you were having dinner with a potential employer, would you not dress your best and use your best table manners? Do these things really not work for the poor? Can the poor really not "fake it to make it"?

I suspect that in many cases they can. David Ellwood tells the story of Eugene Lang, the CEO who in 1980 told a Harlem sixth-grade class that he would pay for the college tuition of any students in the class who successfully graduated from high school. Over the years that followed, the promise-eligible students engaged actively in their studies, and when they did not, there were plenty of engaged parents and teachers around them eager to get them back on track so they would not lose the opportunity.

Of the fifty-one school children in attendance at Lang's speech who remained in the area, forty were expected to attend college at the time of Ellwood's writing. But here's the thing. While Lang did pay for a social worker to support the students as they grew up, he actually had to pay very little to make good on his promise of college tuition. Many of the students received full scholarships, while others attended low-cost colleges nearby.[32]

Ellwood tells this story to show the power of hope for people living in poverty. At the same time, it is hard to see how Lang's speech did anything more than simply invite those students and that community to let go of the false belief they had that attending college was something beyond their reach. The students were able to "fake it" (that their college tuition would be paid for) to "make it" (by attending college).

In Chapter 2, we saw that Charles Karelis's variant of the *contextual* view suggests that the laws of economics for the rich and middle class – in particular the law of marginal utility – do not apply to the poor. That is, it makes no sense to solve one of your problems if you still have hundreds more.

At its most extreme, the *structural* view implies that the poor even live by different laws of the *universe*. For the rich and middle class, thoughts and actions play a significant role in shaping outcomes. You can reprogram your thoughts, you can do "power poses," and you can adopt a "growth mindset" that reframes failure as an opportunity to learn.

For the poor, however, things work differently. There is nothing they can do. Only fundamental structural change can bring about a meaningful improvement in their lives, and it is "pernicious as well as foolish"[33] to believe otherwise. As economists Farwa Sial and Carolina Alves write:

The structural odds against [the poor] inhibit their ability to leave the vicious cycles of poverty. Without additional resources and much more concerted action on the underlying causes, no amount of positive thinking will enable the great mass of individuals to climb out of poverty.[34]

Those holding the *structural* view resist the notion that the poor contribute *at all* to their own poverty because to do so would be to "blame the victim," to concede defeat to the political right, to ignore structural and institutional drivers of poverty, to undermine the political will for social change, and to collaborate with an unjust system. The consequence of this framing – quite paradoxically – is that it disempowers the poor.

It does so in two ways. First, it moves the locus of activity to domains where the poor have no power. Well-meaning organizations engage poor communities in advocating in the halls of power (someone else's, anyway) for the systems-level changes they believe are necessary, diverting the poor's energy away from where they could use it more effectively to address issues in their own lives.

Second, it promotes a narrative of powerlessness in which the poor's efforts to improve their own lives would be of little use anyway. This narrative flies in the face of the positive thinking increasingly embraced by the rich and middle class. It reinforces the fatalism and "fixed mindsets" of the poor, while validating the belief that stress is harmful (which, according to Kelly McGonigal, makes it so). It dismisses the value of one's inner resources in the face of adversity and ignores the possibility that trauma might lead to growth.

As Glenn Loury notes in the context of racial discrimination, though his comments apply to poverty as well, "where failure at a personal level is impossible [because everything's blamed on the 'system'], there can be no personal success." Yet this is precisely the fatalism embodied by Ellwood when he writes:

> Ghetto residents are often accused of thinking only of the present and ignoring the future. It is hard to see how looking to the future would give them more initiative or drive, since the future does not look much different from the past.[35]

The rich and middle class believe that their own futures can be different from their pasts, often subscribing to the adage that "the best way to predict the future is to create it." But it seems that in their efforts to see the poor as fundamentally like themselves, to avoid "othering" the poor, the left has inadvertently turned the poor into something very different indeed. They have excluded the poor from powerful ideas (and even common sense) about the agency we each have in shaping our own reality. In isolating the poor from the behavioral scrutiny of conservatives, the left has reinforced a narrative that isolates the poor from the levers that are most available to them for improving their own lives.

∞

So far in this chapter, I have challenged the visceral resistance of many on the political left to any suggestion that the poor contribute to their own poverty, and I have placed this resistance in the context of trends dating back to the 1960s. But we cannot leave this topic without also addressing the one moment when many of these trends coalesced to produce a trauma for the left that persists to this day.

In March of 1965, assistant secretary of labor Daniel Patrick Moynihan and two associates completed a report intended for a small audience of high-ranking officials in the federal government. His intent in *The Negro Family: A Case for National Action* was to overcome the officials' misplaced optimism that the recently passed civil rights legislation had resolved the issue of African-American equality. To Moynihan, such optimism defied the data on the worsening social and economic circumstances of African-Americans.

Moynihan was also aware that the major initiatives of the War on Poverty, such as community action programs and welfare programs, had failed to address – and may have been counterproductive for – the issue of family structure. As a Catholic and as the product of a fatherless childhood himself, Moynihan saw family structure as central to the "Negro problem" and as the appropriate measure for evaluating the success of government initiatives to address unemployment and poverty.

The "Moynihan Report" quickly became a lightning rod for debates on poverty, and it has remained as such ever since. Within months of its completion, the report prompted "one of the angriest and most bitter controversies yet among government and private individuals all presumably dedicated to realizing Negro rights."[36]

The report captured what white sociologists had long written about the "Negro problem." While it covered a wide range of structural issues like unemployment and discrimination, as well as the historical experience of slavery, it collapsed these issues into the resulting "tangle of pathology" in an African-American family characterized by illegitimacy, matriarchy, and diminished male identity.

The many critiques of Moynihan's report cover everything from the methodology of his analysis to the long-term
consequences of the position he came to personify. In some
cases, he approached the problem in ways that are no longer
socially acceptable, such as his suggestion that employers give
jobs to African-American men (to strengthen their male identities) even if the employers needed to take the jobs away from
African-American women.

These critiques aside, the public never really had a chance to
engage with the report's contents on its own merits. Early press
coverage of the report and the policy conversation to which
it contributed introduced prejudices and misunderstandings
that remain to this day. Mary McGrory from *The Washington
Star* wrote that President Johnson "urged black Americans to
forgive and forget and to look frankly at their own failures,"
and to address the issue of "the breakdown of the Negro family structure." John D. Pomfret of the *New York Times* ignored
the report's discussion of most structural factors and noted that
"the fundamental source of weakness of the Negro community
is the deterioration of the Negro family."[37]

Contrast these depictions with what Johnson had expressed
in a June 1965 speech at Howard University that was co-written
by Moynihan and based on the report: "Perhaps most important – its influence radiating to every part of life – is the breakdown of the Negro family structure. For this, most of all, white
America must accept responsibility."[38] While Johnson clearly
blamed whites, the press coverage redirected that blame at
African-Americans themselves.

In light of this press coverage, and in particular the piece
by Pomfret, the government decided to release the full report
to the public. *Newsweek* published a summary of the report in

early August of 1965, noting that the report had "set off a quiet revolution in the basic White House approach to the continuing American dilemma of race."[39]

External events soon elevated the controversy. Two days after the report's release, riots broke out in the Watts area of Los Angeles after a police officer arrested an African-American man for reckless driving, and rumors spread that in the altercation police had struck a pregnant woman. The five days of rioting that followed caused thirty-four deaths and more than $40 million in property damage.

Public opinion on the riots quickly bifurcated into two perspectives – on one side that African-Americans were unruly and uncivilized, and on the other that the riots were an understandable and predictable response to the social and economic hardships of the black ghetto. In this context, people increasingly came to see the Moynihan Report as the government statement of the former. As Susan Greenbaum writes, "Framed as a policy document to help uplift poor black families and correct the effects of past discrimination, [the Moynihan Report] came to be regarded by both supporters and detractors as an indictment of African American culture, a pessimistic warning that legal rights and safety net programs would not be enough."[40]

The Moynihan Report is largely responsible for the racialization of the "culture of poverty" construct in the collective imagination of the political left. The national trauma brought about by the riots in Watts and in other urban centers indelibly linked Moynihan's notion of an African-American "tangle of pathology" to Lewis's previously race-independent notion of a "culture of poverty."

And yet, is the Moynihan Report really about race? For all the focus on African-American family structure, the report marshals data to show that broken homes were a consequence of unemployment, with a one-year lag, rather than its cause. Further, the report makes clear that nearly half of African-American families by that time had entered the middle class, and that these families adhered *more closely* to middle-class values (e.g., limited family size, financial thrift) than did white middle-class families. And for all the attention to the "three centuries of sometimes unimaginable mistreatment [that] have taken their toll" on African-Americans,[41] the report shows that the black family was more intact in the rural South than it was in the Northern cities to which many African-Americans had migrated throughout the 20th century. One could argue that a more apt title for the report may have been, "Low-Skill Employment: The Case for National Action," or "Social Effects of the 'Great Migration.'"

After more than fifty years of angst over the content and perception of the Moynihan Report, we can hopefully now disentangle the "culture of poverty" construct from the issue of race so that we can have a more productive conversation about the role the poor play in perpetuating their own poverty. The "culture of poverty" is not a racial construct. In fact, to the extent that Moynihan documented a "tangle of pathology" in African-American families, he was far less effective in showing that the pathology was *unique* to African-American families. Later in 1965 Moynihan wrote:

> From the wild Irish slums of the 19th century eastern seaboard, to the riot-torn suburbs of Los Angeles, there is one unmistakable lesson in American history; a community that allows a large number of men to grow up in broken families, dominated by women, never acquiring

any stable relationship to male authority, never acquiring any set of rational expectations about the future – that community asks for and gets chaos.[42]

This statement echoes Lewis's view that such community attributes exist independently of racial identity or historical experience. This is the premise on which our discussion of the "culture of poverty" is based, in the hope that it allows readers to engage with the *cultural* explanation of poverty without projecting onto it the racialized version contained – or believed to be contained – in the Moynihan Report. The "culture of poverty," when applied equally across all racial and ethnic groups, provides a useful lens (though not the only lens, for sure) on behaviors of the poor that people in all four quadrants of our framework can acknowledge.

∞

As humans, we all contribute to our own life outcomes. While appropriately drawing attention to the systemic factors of poverty, the *structural* view tends to ignore the genuine agency the poor have in improving their own lives. In the U.S., this has arguably disempowered the poor while at the same time it has undermined political support for the structural reforms that holders of this view have sought.

Hopefully, this exploration of the history of this dynamic has helped the reader relax any visceral resistance to the notion that the poor contribute – at least in some way – to their own poverty, as notoriously suggested by the "culture of poverty" construct. If so, then we are ready to explore the possibility that all four of the quadrants may have some validity of their own.

CHAPTER FOUR

CAN THEY ALL BE TRUE?

"The test of a first-rate intelligence is the ability to hold two opposed ideas in the mind at the same time, and still retain the ability to function."

F. Scott Fitzgerald

In the preceding chapters, I surveyed four prevailing explanations of poverty, and unlike most other authors, I focused not on which view is right but on the full scope of each perspective and on the emotions that might lead one to adopt it. I have offered my own guesses in that regard, which may be accurate for some people and inaccurate for others. I invite those holding one of these perspectives to decide for themselves whether I got it right or whether their emotional experience is different from what I suggest. Even if I am wrong, I hope my assertions will prompt readers to look more closely at their emotional attachments to their beliefs.

Each one of these four perspectives offers a limited understanding of poverty; it offers part of the truth, but not all of the truth. Common sense deems this to be so. Somewhere there is a poor and pregnant teenager who really should have known better. Somewhere a hardworking man cannot find a job with a living wage. Somewhere the "decision fatigue" that comes with poverty is eroding a mother's ability to care for her children the way she knows she should. Somewhere a father is inculcating his daughter with "hidden rules" of life that will not serve her over the long term.

We have difficulty allowing all these things to be true at the same time. That we feel the need to collapse poverty into only one of these four perspectives is an epistemological problem we will address in the next chapter. *Which* of the perspectives we choose follows from how we interpret the logic of each perspective in the emotional context of our own lives. We tend to adopt the perspectives that reflect, justify, and reinforce the emotions we already feel, and to reject the perspectives within which those emotions would be out of place.

But we can challenge this collapsing tendency by reframing how we think about each dimension of our framework. I have arranged the four perspectives along these two dimensions: whether the poor person is more similar to the observer (a "self") or different from the observer (an "other"); and whether poverty is an individual circumstance or a systemic or environmental phenomenon.

For both dimensions, researchers have conducted many studies to prove that the answer is one or the other. But what if it's actually both? When we think of each dimension not as a problem to solve through research, but as a polarity or a tension to manage, we gain access to the insights of all four quadrants.

According to Barry Johnson,[1] a polarity is a question to which there are two or more valid answers. When facing a polarity, the goal is not to collapse to the "best" answer but rather to maximize the upsides of all valid answers while minimizing their downsides.

Let us look first at the dimension of "self" versus "other." Common sense tells me that the poor are in some ways very much like me, and in other ways quite unlike me. As Clyde Kluckhohn and Henry A. Murray write, "Every man is in certain respects (a) like all other men, (b) like some other men, [and] (c) like no other man."[2] Remarkably, much of the debate over the "culture of poverty" has turned on whether the attitudes, values, and behaviors of the poor are sufficiently distinct from the mainstream to be viewed as a culture in their own right. It just depends where you draw the line.

When we view the poor as a "self," as fundamentally like us, then we more easily empathize with their situation. We focus on what all people have in common, and we can see their unfulfilled potential. However, we may ignore the role they play in creating their own life outcomes or we may falsely assume that they have everything they need to be successful – if only we could remove the structures and stresses of poverty. But if you deny a person's culpability for being where they are, then you also deny their agency for getting to somewhere better.[3]

When we view the poor as an "other," as fundamentally different from us, we stand up for behavioral norms that lead to individual and societal success and we can attend to the attitudinal and cultural factors that may lead the poor not to conform. However, we may blame the poor by exaggerating their role in their predicaments, and we may come to see them as fundamentally unable to be successful on our terms. We may ultimately cut them off from both our sentiments and our support.

Let us now turn to the dimension of individual circumstance versus systemic or environmental phenomenon. Again, common sense tells me that both are in some way true. I make my own decisions, but I do so in a larger structural and cultural context that shapes both the decisions I make and the outcomes they produce.

When we view poverty as an individual circumstance, we recognize the uniqueness of each person's situation and we can work with the individuals to identify concrete, near-term actions they could take to improve their own outcomes. However, we may overlook genuine barriers that the poor face, and we may inadvertently undermine the political will to remove those barriers. Policy preferences that emphasize the role of the individual may leave vulnerable groups unsupported, particularly those our personalized efforts have not yet reached.

When we view poverty as a systemic or environmental phenomenon, we acknowledge the structural and cultural contexts that shape individual decisions and their consequences, and we produce clear messaging to garner support for policies with large-scale potential impact. However, we may inadvertently disempower the poor *and* undermine political support for change by propagating a narrative that the poor cannot improve their lives (at all) on their own. Further, we may distract the poor from improving their own lives by enlisting them in policy debates where they have little power. At worst, the poor may become props in a political argument they do not fully understand.

At this point, it suffices to recognize that each side of each dimension has both upsides and downsides. By taking on each of the four perspectives – at least temporarily – we can maximize the upsides, minimize the downsides, and gain new insights on our efforts to reduce poverty.

For several years I have led an exercise for my graduate

students in social enterprise, in which I ask them to consider a social challenge they have chosen to work on from all four perspectives. Given the emotional dynamics discussed so far, it should come as no surprise that many students find this experience quite stressful and disconcerting.

And yet, they derive important insights from the process, and many students have reframed their challenges and come up with more robust and sophisticated interventions as a result. By taking on all four perspectives, they see into their previous blind spots regarding the people and contexts with which they seek to work. You can use this exercise to strengthen your own efforts to reduce poverty by exploring the questions in **Figure 2**.

System/Environment

STRUCTURAL	CULTURAL
What obstacles prevent individuals from obtaining better outcomes?	How might the challenge reflect deeper attitudinal or behavioral patterns that persist across generations?
What actions might one take to remove those obstacles or improve the structures?	What actions might one take to disrupt or supplant those patterns?
How are certain groups systematically deprived of the opportunity to obtain better outcomes?	What positive practices have already emerged within the community that could be highlighted and expanded?
How do multiple obstacles reinforce one another to "trap" the people concerned?	How might multiple generations be engaged in the solution?

Self ← — — — — — — — — — — — — — — — — — → Other

CONTEXTUAL	BEHAVIORAL
How might people's seemingly unhelpful behaviors make sense within their particular context?	How are the people experiencing the challenge actually contributing to it?
How might the stress effects of scarcity (e.g., "bandwidth tax," "decision fatigue") foster adverse outcomes?	What incentives promote these counterproductive behaviors?
How might one shift the context?	What actions might one take to eliminate these behaviors?
How might one "nudge" people toward more constructive behaviors?	How might one incentivize behaviors that would be more helpful?

Individual

Figure 2.

Even conducting this brief exercise may evoke difficult emotions. After all, we choose our preferred quadrant for a reason: it suits the emotion we bring to the poverty conversation. Further, that emotion has focused our perceptive capacity on information that justifies our feelings and reinforces our points of view, so the other quadrants may strike us as not just unsettling, but flatly untrue. So, understanding in cognitive terms that these dimensions are "polarities" rather than "problems" is not enough. We must also release the emotions that led us to make our choices in the first place.

Philosopher Jean-Paul Sartre suggests that we turn to emotion when we feel overwhelmed by the task we are expected to perform, when we do not believe we will be able to complete it.[4] By exhibiting an emotion, we disrupt the calm that we would need in order to complete the task, and we construct a worldview that accounts for our failure. If Sartre is correct, then what is the task we feel we cannot do that gives rise to each of the emotions I have associated with the various quadrants: pride, guilt, fear, disgust, frustration, anger, and despair?

Pride allows us to avoid the fact that our successes derive, to a great extent, from forces beyond our control. Sure, we all do our best, but the consequences we face in life rarely correspond precisely to the actions we take. In all things, we are subject to the vagaries of life. As J.D. Vance writes of his escape from poverty and family dysfunction, on the way to a law degree from Yale and a successful financial career (not to mention a best-selling memoir):

> Thinking about it now, about how close I was to the abyss, gives me the chills. I am one lucky son of a bitch."[5]

Guilt takes several forms in the poverty arena. The first is the simple guilt of being better off than others for reasons we cannot readily identify. Like the pride discussed above, perhaps this guilt helps us avoid accepting the fact that we are subject to random forces that shape our lives. We assume responsibility for outcomes that are beyond our control.

Second, there is the guilt that comes from having done things we now regret in order to get where we are today. This guilt helps us avoid making amends and restoring our relationships with those we have harmed – similar to what is described in steps 4, 8, and 9 of the Alcoholics Anonymous 12-step program: "Made a searching and fearless moral inventory of ourselves"; "Made a list of all persons we had harmed, and became willing to make amends to them all"; and "Made direct amends to such people wherever possible, except when to do so would injure them or others."[6]

The third type of guilt combines the other two. We may feel guilty that our forebears engaged in activities we find abhorrent, such as colonization and slavery, in order to shape reality unfairly in their favor and ours. To some extent, their actions have nothing to do with us; we were born into a privileged position through no fault of our own. At the same time, the question remains: Do we hold within us the vestiges of the attitudes and motivations that led our forebears to act as they did? Processing this kind of guilt may require *both* a "searching and fearless moral inventory of ourselves" *and* a willingness to let go of the feeling of responsibility for things we did not do.

Fear seems pretty clear-cut; it reminds us that we might lose something – our money, our loved ones, our own lives. Fear helps us avoid accepting the inherent uncertainty of the future and living as boldly as we can nonetheless. Fear *of others* helps us avoid living boldly in our relationships with people very much unlike ourselves.

As for disgust, researchers distinguish between physical disgust, which is evoked by things like dead animals, rancid meat, and bodily fluids, and sociomoral disgust, which we internalize from our cultures. Physical disgust, which you might feel when walking past a homeless person who reeks of urine, reminds us of our animal nature. In particular, physical disgust reminds us that we will die. No matter how intelligent or inspired we believe ourselves to be, there is no escape.

Sociomoral disgust triggers our cultural learning that a certain person is an "other." Charles Darwin made the first modern scientific observation about disgust when he wrote:

> In Tierra del Fuego a native touched with his fingers some cold preserved meat which I was eating at our bivouac and plainly showed utter disgust at its softness; whilst I felt utter disgust at my food being touched by a naked savage, though his hands did not appear dirty.[7]

Because we culturally learn sociomoral disgust, there is no substance behind the emotion. To define someone as an "other" (or worse, a "savage") *is* to mark the person as a source of disgust. Sociomoral disgust does not protect us *per se*; it simply helps us avoid interacting with people and things our forebears found unfamiliar.

Our last three emotions seem to relate to the effort to reduce or eradicate poverty. Frustration is the feeling we get when our continuous efforts do not achieve the results we have in mind. Frustration helps us avoid the task of looking ever more deeply into ourselves to discover what needs to change in us – and in what we are doing – so that we can be more effective in meeting our goals. In Chapter 2, we noted the frustration of the *contextual* view, which strives for simple solutions to poverty ("a little bit of well-targeted help"[8]) and thus assumes *a priori* that "the poor must know what they are doing."[9]

Despair is the emotion that allows us to give up completely. This emotion helps us avoid taking action when the impact of our efforts is uncertain. In this vein, I suspect that the current aspiration to "eradicate poverty in our lifetimes" is a bit too ambitious. It sets us up for despair if our initial efforts prove unsuccessful. Our feelings of despair would then lead us to stop soldiering on when the task turns out to be more difficult than we had thought.

I have mixed feelings about anger. As Paul Ekman notes, "Anger at injustice motivates actions to bring about change."[10] Anger alerts us to features of our world that we consider unjust, and motivates us to fight to make them right. At the same time, when anger is directed toward specific people who are considered culpable for the world's ills, it often prompts defensiveness and even greater resistance to change.

Perhaps the best advice about anger comes from Mohandas Gandhi:

> I have learnt through bitter experience the one supreme lesson: to conserve my anger, and as heat conserved is transmuted into energy, even so our anger controlled can be transmuted into a power which can move the world.[11]

What Gandhi describes may no longer be anger as we typically understand it – anger we unleash on those who have done us harm. This is a slow-burning anger that steels the nerves, cultivates confidence in one's purpose, and focuses the mind on action. But as Brazilian educationalist Paulo Freire writes, that action cannot be simply to turn the tables on one's oppressor. One must act out of a love that can free both the oppressed and the oppressor from the underlying dynamic of oppression.[12]

This review of the emotions considered thus far suggests that what keeps us in our current way of thinking about poverty (no matter which quadrant we choose) is everything we hope to avoid. We avoid the hard reality that we are fundamentally subject to the vagaries of life, that we do things we will eventually regret, and that the future is inherently uncertain except for the certainty that we will die. We avoid the recognition that our efforts during our lifetimes may not have the impact we desire, and that our greatest impact may come from how we change ourselves.

What if we could reframe poverty in a way that accepted all those hard-to-accept realities as its basic premises? Such a way of thinking would eliminate the need to go into all those emotions in the first place. We could then maximize the upsides and minimize the downsides of the existing perspectives on poverty – not by managing the tensions among them on an ongoing basis but by crafting a broader way of thinking about poverty that integrates the valid aspects of each. We could then become more potent change leaders by resolving the conflicts and inconsistencies brought about by our emotional commitment to a limited understanding.

Crafting this broader way of thinking about poverty will be our focus in Part Two.

PART TWO

CHAPTER FIVE

WE'VE BEEN ASKING THE WRONG QUESTIONS

"Natural science does not simply describe and explain nature; it is a part of the interplay between nature and ourselves; it describes nature as exposed to our method of questioning."

Werner Heisenberg

In 1687, Isaac Newton published his *Philosophiae Naturalis Principia Mathematica*. In the groundbreaking text, he presented three laws that govern the motion of objects in the physical world. These laws state that:

1. Every object persists in its state of rest or uniform motion in a straight line unless it is compelled to change that state by forces impressed on it.

2. Force is equal to the change in momentum per change in time. For a constant mass, force equals mass times acceleration.

3. For every action, there is an equal and opposite reaction.

Newton's three laws allow for systematic exploration of countless phenomena from a deterministic perspective that links causes to their effects. This worldview was perhaps best expressed by Pierre Simon, Marquis de Laplace, who in 1814 wrote that "We may regard the present state of the universe as the effect of its past and the cause of its future." Laplace argued that an intellect who knew the position and movement of every particle in the universe would be able to predict any past, present, or future state.[1]

Over the several centuries since Newton published his *Principia*, scientists have applied this deterministic approach to a growing range of problems. Their understanding of the forces that lead from cause to effect in a wide variety of settings have vastly improved our understanding of our universe and have led to inventions like "the telephone and the radio, the automobile and the airplane, the phonograph and the moving pictures, the turbine and the diesel engine, and the modern hydroelectric power plant."[2]

Newtonian determinism has also shaped our understanding of social systems and the interactions that occur within them. In an effort to become more rigorous, the social sciences adopted this way of thinking and sought to mimic the methodologies that had proven so useful in the physical sciences. For example, the randomized controlled trials championed by behavioral economists Banerjee and Duflo seek to isolate individual potential causes and measure their effects. Researchers then extrapolate those cause-and-effect relationships to settings where the factors are not so isolated.

The limits of Newtonianism have become apparent as scientists have explored new areas like systems theory, quantum mechanics, complexity science, and chaos. Speaking to the Royal Society on the 300th anniversary of Newton's *Principia*, British mathematician Sir James Lighthill said:

We [practitioners of mechanics] are all deeply conscious today that the enthusiasm of our forebears for the marvelous achievements of Newtonian mechanics led them to make generalizations in this area of predictability which, indeed, we may have generally tended to believe before 1960, but which we now recognize were false. We collectively wish to apologize for having misled the general educated public by spreading ideas about the determinism of systems satisfying Newton's laws of motion that, after 1960, were to be proved incorrect.[3]

However, Newtonianism still provides the basic framing of our poverty discourse. We can see this by using the metaphor of a simple problem that high school physics teachers often use to introduce their students to Newton's three laws of motion. The problem consists of a ball moving along a linear surface. Students apply the three laws to calculate what happens to the ball as various forces act upon it. Maybe another ball comes along and strikes it, transferring some of its own momentum in the process, or maybe the friction of the surface slows it down.

Figure 3 illustrates the four perspectives discussed in Chapter 2 in terms of this simple physics problem. Imagine that the person experiencing poverty can be represented by a ball sitting on the wrong side of an arbitrary "poverty line." The actual value of this line will, of course, vary. It may represent the World Bank's $1.90 per day, the federal poverty level in the U.S., or some other line defined for a different country or context.

To escape poverty, the ball must cross this line. Whether or not it will do so depends on the answers to two questions: First,

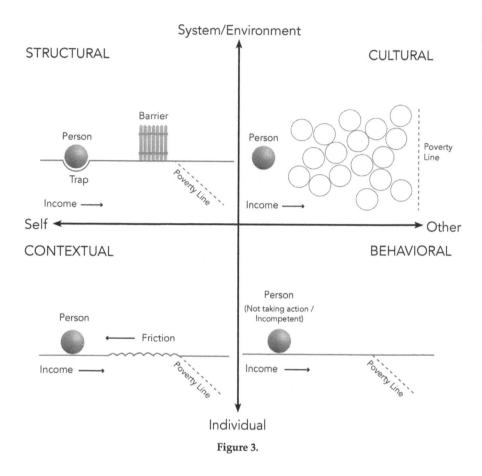

Figure 3.

is the ball moving or is it at rest? That is, is the person moving out of poverty on his or her own, or just sitting still? Second, are there any external forces that may act upon it? That is, does the person have a clear, linear route out of poverty, or are there obstacles or other forces impeding the way?

In the *behavioral* quadrant, the route may be clear, but the ball is not moving. It just sits there. To get it moving, one must exert force upon it (e.g., through work requirements for social benefits) or just give up hope (e.g., by cutting such benefits). In the *cultural* quadrant, seen here in an overhead view, the ball is not moving because it is held back by the other balls around it – that is, by members of its community who reinforce a poverty mindset. In the *structural* quadrant, the ball may be trying to move, but either it is stuck in a poverty trap or it is blocked by barriers such as low wages or institutionalized discrimination. In the *contextual* quadrant, the ball may be trying to move, but the forces of friction – that is, the stresses associated with being poor – consistently hold it back.

How might one conceptualize this first question of whether or not the ball is moving? A few terms from the poverty literature come to mind: personal responsibility, competence, and rationality. While these terms are not synonymous, they are no doubt related.

Haskins and Sawhill define personal responsibility to mean "that individuals must make decisions and take actions that promote their own growth and well-being as well as that of their children."[4] This seems to indicate an *intention* to take care of oneself, though it does not rule out that the efforts may be inhibited by forces beyond one's control. But the person exercising personal responsibility will keep trying nonetheless.

Lawrence Mead writes about competence, which refers to individuals' *ability* to organize their own lives and to take care of their own material needs. Mead argues that the best indicator of competence is a person's willingness to work.[5] This sounds like personal responsibility (e.g., the intention to take care of oneself) with some basic skills added in. The competent person may not have the knowledge and job skills to escape poverty, but presumably can learn these things if trained.

Rationality, in economics, refers to a set of classical assumptions about human behavior, particularly that economic actors seek to maximize utility. In psychology, the term refers to a logic underlying one's cognitive process in which he or she makes decisions for reasons. Rationality is the key component of competence as Mead defines it. (Later I will suggest that some people may be competent without being rational, but we can ignore this for now.)

For now, let us just use the term rationality to capture whether or not the ball is moving, recognizing that it is related to – but not synonymous with – terms like competence and personal responsibility that we should also consider as part of the discussion. Rationality has the advantage of referring to a discrete cognitive process taking place within the person, whereas the other terms capture more amorphous factors that also contribute to a person's outcomes. Further, rationality appears consistently in the poverty literature across all four quadrants.

Until now, we have defined the horizontal dimension of our two-by-two framework in terms of whether the observer of poverty sees the person experiencing poverty as a "self" or as an "other." I now propose that what makes someone seem like a "self" is that we assess them to be rational in the sense described above. If we view ourselves as rational, then we will see others who seem rational as much like us, leading us to believe that we would do the same as them if we were in their shoes. People who behave differently in the same situation confuse us, leading us to view them as irrational and thus fundamentally different from us. The emotional assessment ("self" versus "other") corresponds to the objective assessment (rational versus irrational).

When we look at how each quadrant addresses rationality, we see that it mirrors what we've already said about the ball's motion in our physics problem.

The *structural* view assumes that the poor are rational

without a particularly good reason for doing so. Amartya Sen writes that "the people have to be seen, in this perspective, as being actively involved – given the opportunity – in shaping their own destiny."[6] The only unknown variable is the level of opportunity ("capabilities") available for them to pursue.

Wolff and de-Shalit define a "genuine opportunity" as one for which "it is reasonable to expect [a person] to take steps to achieve that functioning."[7] But what if the reasonableness of the person with the expectation does not *also* exist in the mind of the person who is expected to take the action?

The *structural* view creates its own blind spot by projecting the observer's rationality onto the person observed. It assumes that the ball is of the type that moves on its own, since the observer is that type of ball. The risk, of course, is that those taking this view will keep on clearing the ball's path of obstacles, only to find that some balls stay where they are. (And *then* what?)

The *contextual* view projects rationality onto the poor and then bends the laws of economics to make their behaviors make sense. For Karelis, that means asserting that different laws of economics apply to the poor than to the rich: It makes sense that the poor do not solve their own problems since they would still have so many more problems left to solve. For brain scientists like Mullainathan and Shafir, it means attributing seemingly irrational behavior to the effects of stress that the obviously rational rich and middle class also endure under similar, though less severe, circumstances.

Banerjee and Duflo just take the poor's rationality as a starting point and then count on their empirical research to tell them why the poor still act as they do:

> What is striking is that even people who are that poor [living on $0.99 PPP[8] per day] are just like

the rest of us in almost every way. We have the same desires and weaknesses; the poor are no less rational than anyone else – quite the contrary. Precisely because they have so little, we often find them putting much careful thought into their choices.[9]

This assumption forces Banerjee and Duflo to explain some irrational behaviors, like workers spending money on expensive festivals rather than on extra food that would improve their productivity,[10] or mothers refusing to pay a few cents to deworm their children even though statistically it would increase their children's lifetime earnings by hundreds of dollars.[11]

Ultimately, Banerjee and Duflo's assumption breaks down. By suggesting that the poor lack the "idea that there is a future" as well as the "mental space" to take a longer view of their lives,[12] they question the rationality of the poor without saying so explicitly. Their theoretical assumption that the ball is moving cannot withstand the empirical finding that its position has not changed.

For the *behavioral* view, to argue that the behaviors associated with poverty fit any common notion of rationality strains the meaning of the word. As Mead writes:

Unless rationality involves foresight, it is not distinguishable from impulse, and unless the goal maximized involves material gain, then all behavior becomes rational, in the sense that some purpose lies behind it.[13]

Unlike the *structural* and *contextual* views, this view asserts that the poor behave irrationally due to a deficiency either of innate capacity or of motivation, and that this perpetuates their poverty. The downside of this view is that actual barriers blocking the path of a ball at rest will tend to be ignored.

The *cultural* view sees irrationality as a logic in its own right, and as a cultural adaptation that helps the poor person navigate his environment and avoid being overwhelmed by misery. The poor behave irrationally, but consistently and predictably so.

The risk of this view is that it assumes that this irrationality is a cultural trait that will never change. It ignores the possibility that the ball may, at some point in time, start moving on its own. As Oscar Lewis writes:

> By the time slum children are six or seven they have usually absorbed the basic attitudes and values of their subculture. Thereafter they are psychologically unready to take full advantage of changing conditions or improving opportunities that may develop in their lifetime.[14]

Many policy decisions related to poverty depend on how one answers this question of whether or not the ball is moving. If it is, then policy should seek to free it from any traps and to eliminate the barriers and friction that impede its path. If not, then policy must act upon it like an external force, with programs that create incentives for it to start moving, or it should simply leave the ball where it is and minimize the hassle and expense for everyone else. In the latter case, Charles Murray seems to invoke Newton's third law that every action has an equal and opposite reaction – that is, providing unconditional support to the non-working poor may undermine broadly held norms of personal responsibility. Dambisa Moyo makes a similar point regarding the corrupting effect of foreign aid to poor countries in Africa: "Aid supports rent-seeking – that is, the use of governmental authority to take and make money without trade or production of wealth."[15]

I have not said as much about the second question – about traps, barriers, and forces – in part because the answer to this question often follows the answer to the first. If the poor behave rationally, then there must be *something else* keeping them poor. If the poor behave irrationally, then addressing traps, barriers, and forces is a waste of time – at least for now. Once the poor have achieved rationality, one can address the obstacles that may be making their escape from poverty more difficult.

The four different explanations of poverty we have explored – *behavioral, structural, contextual,* and *cultural* – answer these questions in different ways. These are the stories we have created to explain poverty, and the stories follow the rules of the Newtonian determinism we have all been taught. We seem to have accepted the premise of the high school physics problem; we just set up the problem differently.

We then engage in a competitive discourse with those who have set up the problem differently. We challenge the knowledge, intelligence, and even the sincerity of our opponents in the other quadrants. We have done this for several centuries at least, and the resulting discourse has done little to deepen our fundamental understanding of poverty.

The problem, of course, is not that any of us has answered these questions incorrectly, but rather that they are the wrong questions in the first place. We have derived the questions from a way of thinking that, as seen in Sir James Lighthill's apology above, has been proven false. But what's wrong with the questions?

First, rationality is not something that some people have

and other people do not. At birth, none of us is rational. We only become rational – perhaps – later in life.

Second, the world is not linear. The path out of poverty is not a straight line that we must simply clear of obstacles. It is complex and ever-changing, and a small difference can make a huge impact on the final outcome.

CHAPTER SIX

THE VAGARIES OF LIFE

"My momma always said life was like a box of chocolates.
You never know what you're gonna get."

Forrest Gump, in *Forrest Gump*

Part One began with an interview in which Ben Carson claimed that those in poverty have the "wrong mindset." Later in the same interview, Carson reflected on his own rise from poverty and on one factor that had, in his view, proven critical to his success:

> If everybody had a mother like mine, nobody would be in poverty. She was a person who absolutely would not accept the status of victim.[1]

It is a startling claim – that one person could have had so great an impact on his life outcomes, especially in light of all the challenges he must have faced along the way. But such claims are common in the poverty literature. David Ellwood makes the general point that "those who do [make it out of poverty] usually had a strong determination and some significant figure in their life who guided them and encouraged them to rise above their world."[2]

What are we to make of Carson's comment about his mother, and of other personal stories that place such emphasis on one person as the linchpin for getting out of poverty? From a Newtonian perspective, we may want to ask: *Is this all it takes?* Is having an encouraging mother who refuses to accept the status of victim the key to escaping poverty?

If so, then other poor mothers should encourage their children more. Perhaps the government could create training programs to teach mothers how to do it. This sounds bizarre, but it is not too far a stretch from programs that some have introduced to offset "cultural deprivation" within the home.[3]

Alternatively, perhaps Carson is an "outlier" – a data point so far from the norm that his experience offers little insight about the overall path out of poverty. In that case, we can dismiss his comment about his mother. As urban policy professor Mindy Fullilove says of Carson's comments:

> One of the hallmarks of science is that we are taught not to overgeneralize from a single case ... The case is always true, but there's always variation. So the fact that he [Carson] as an individual – or I – could get out of poverty and go to medical school and have successful careers doesn't mean anybody who's in poverty could.[4]

Thus, though we can acknowledge Carson's mother's role, we can also see that other mothers encourage their children too

– or want to – but that the traps, barriers, and stresses of poverty
are often just too great. One might even suggest that it is cruel to
encourage a poor child, since it may build up expectations that,
in the majority of cases, can never be fulfilled. As development
economist Seema Jayachandran writes:

> While moderately high aspirations can pro-
> vide crucial motivation, unrealistically high as-
> pirations can be so discouraging that they are
> harmful. Repeatedly falling short can deplete
> motivation.[5]

For most of the years since Newton published his *Principia*,
scientists believed that small differences, like having a particularly encouraging mother, did not matter. The scientist's job was
to describe the fundamental laws by which the universe oper-
ated. Copernicus described how the planets revolve around
the sun, Kepler drew their elliptical orbits, and Newton told us
how objects move here on Earth.

Their laws provided models of "linear" systems that are
relatively easy to comprehend. Linear systems have two essential properties. First, the system behaves the same across all
scales, from the very big to the very small. Second, the system's
response to a sum of inputs is equal to the sum of its response
to each input individually; any interaction among the inputs
can be ignored. Given these properties, a small difference in the
initial conditions or a small perturbation along the way will not
significantly change the system's final state.

Applying this way of thinking to Ben Carson's situation, we
might assume that the encouragement one receives from one's
mother, in the grand scheme of things, plays an insignificant

role in the person's escape from poverty. There are far bigger factors to contend with: a global economy, an education system, institutional racism, etc. What can a mother really do?

We now know that the assumption that small differences do not matter no longer holds in all cases. Scientists working across multiple disciplines in what came to be called "chaos theory" and "complexity science" shook this belief as they explored systems that were "nonlinear." In nonlinear systems, the whole is *more* than the sum of its parts – interaction among the parts can yield surprising outcomes.

As an example of a nonlinear system, let's explore how the population of a species changes over time.[6] In a given habitat, the ultimate value of a population will vary based on the birth rate, the death rate, and the "carrying capacity" of the habitat (the maximum population that the habitat can support). For simplicity, let's combine these three variables into one, which we will call r. (See **Figure 4.**)

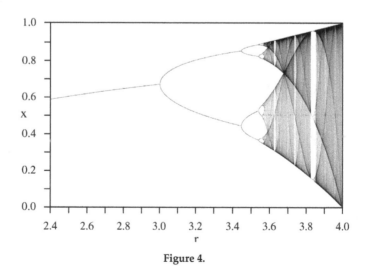

Figure 4.

At low values of r, the population will stabilize at some level, X, that we can calculate ahead of time, and it will be the same for *any* initial population size. No matter where the population starts, it will move toward a level as high as the habitat will allow.

As r increases, things get more interesting. The population level starts flipping back and forth between values – back and forth, year by year. First, it oscillates between two values, then four values, then eight, etc. Again, the population function follows the same pattern regardless of the initial population size.

As r increases further, the behavior of the population function reaches a point where it no longer provides the same outcome (whether fixed or oscillating) for all initial population sizes. Even a small difference in the initial level can produce a wide variation in the population size at some later point in time. At this level of r, the population function yields chaos.

The dichotomous Newtonian explanations of Ben Carson's comment – that is, that most poor mothers do not encourage their children, or that Carson's success is an outlier – both assume that the path out of poverty is linear, like the high school physics problem presented earlier. According to that metaphor, a mother's encouragement either moves a child toward the "poverty line" (in which case, other poor mothers should encourage their children more) or it does not (in which case Carson's comment is an endearing but irrelevant sentiment). The only remaining question is whether or not there are countervailing barriers that might block the well-encouraged child.

But unlike the physics problem, life is nonlinear. Small differences in initial conditions *do* greatly impact the final outcomes. The self-respect Carson's mother instilled in him as he grew up may well have been key to his success later in life. To understand how this could be so, we need a new metaphor for thinking about the path out of poverty. The high school physics problem no longer works.

If life is nonlinear, then we need a metaphor that allows small differences early on to make a big difference in outcomes. Consider Plinko, the carnival game where you drop a disc from the top of a pegboard and it tumbles downward toward a resting place at the bottom of the board, changing direction depending on how it impacts different pegs along the way. (See **Figure 5**.) The place at the top of the board where you drop the disc can represent the circumstances of one's birth, and where the disc ends up at the bottom of the board can represent one's life outcomes.

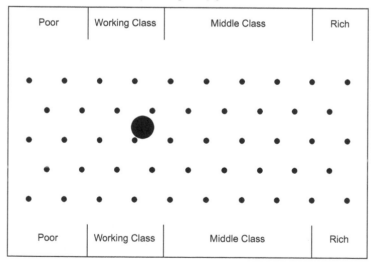

Figure 5.

Using that metaphor, Carson's mother's encouragement could matter a great deal, as a constant force nudging a young Ben Carson slightly to the right each time he reached a new peg – that is, each time he encountered difficulty as he grew up. The cumulative effect of these nudges over the course of his childhood could be enormous.

What else could affect how the disc travels down the Plinko board? Perhaps some pegs have been replaced by ramps. Early childhood education and need-based college scholarships may serve as ramps toward the more favorable outcomes on the right, while poverty itself may act as a ramp to the left by reducing a person's executive functioning, attention span, and emotional self-control through stress,[7] or by stunting intelligence through malnutrition.[8]

One can also imagine semi-porous one- or two-way boundaries that inhibit movement to the left and right – not as simplistically as in the high school physics problem, but at least in ways that are statistically significant. For example, a college fund may inhibit (but not preclude) a middle-class child's drop into poverty, while the lack of access to elite social networks may inhibit the child's movement into the upper class. A basic guaranteed income would create a relatively solid boundary on everyone's left.

As a metaphor for understanding poverty, the Plinko board improves upon the high school physics problem in several respects. The disc is always falling; in no case does it sit motionless. Poor people *are* moving through events in their lives, whether those events route them out of poverty or not. Each event changes their situation in some respect, implying a much wider range of possible interventions than simply trying to get a ball rolling. But since time – like gravity on the Plinko board

– is relentlessly pulling the person toward an outcome, time is of the essence.

The role of time suggests that interventions early in life, or near the top of the board, offer a greater potential impact on life outcomes than interventions later on. A little initial momentum to the right can make a big difference over the life course. This accounts for the justified enthusiasm for early childhood education as an opportunity to reduce poverty.

Through policy, we can change the composition of the Plinko board. We can add or remove pegs, ramps, and boundaries to shape the routes the disc will take down the board. But it will always be a Plinko board. Life will always be nonlinear. Everyone's path will be different, and small differences along the way will matter.

This may dishearten those who hope to eradicate poverty by addressing its so-called "root causes" – by removing the barriers or pushing the ball across the line. As we have seen, it is not that simple.

By the same token, the Plinko board draws our attention to the many places we can intervene along the life course. When life is governed by chance, it means you always have a chance. And you never know when a very small action will have a very big impact.

A very small action had a very big impact on my father, who as I mentioned in Chapter 1 grew up in poverty in rural upstate New York. As he recounts:

> The voice that kept me from a life of pumping gas, or work similar to what my dad had done, was my 10th grade English teacher's saying to me, "You need to go to college," after some writing

assignment I had done in his class. Though it did not seem affordable, and wasn't for me until I got out of the Marines, that little bit of mentoring back in 10th grade greatly influenced my decision to apply to go to [the State University of New York College at] Geneseo.[9]

Imagine the impact that this one comment had on my father's life, on my life, and even on the lives of my children. To say that my family line moved out of poverty *because* of this teacher's comment is probably going too far. But the fact that this one comment stands out in my father's memory more than sixty years after the fact suggests that it played an important role in his life, as I'm sure the encouragement Ben Carson received from his mother did in his.

Small differences matter.

∞

Small differences in initial conditions may help us account for large differences in outcomes on a global scale as well. In *Guns, Germs, and Steel,* Jared Diamond seeks to understand why European civilizations were able to achieve such dominance over other civilizations all over the world.[10] He traces Europeans' success back through history to the climate and to the plant and animal species available to their forebears in Mesopotamia's "Fertile Crescent."

Diamond shows that the plant species native to the Fertile Crescent, when domesticated, offered more productive food sources than plant species found elsewhere. Similarly, Diamond notes that of the fourteen animal species ever domesticated by humans for food or for labor, five of them were native to the Fertile Crescent: the goat, pig, sheep, horse, and cow. The forebears of European civilization, Diamond argues, benefited from a huge geographical advantage over other civilizations emerging elsewhere.

In a linear world, having access to better plant and animal species might not have been a big deal. Sure, Europeans might have grown a little taller or plumper, or they might have had more free time since animals were doing more of their work, but otherwise their outcomes would not differ significantly from those of other civilizations. One might also expect any such differences to disappear once globalization had made those same foods available to everybody.

But the development of civilization is nonlinear. As on a Plinko board, small differences early on can have a huge impact on how societies develop over long periods of time. Higher crop yields in the Fertile Crescent allowed the people living there to feed themselves without needing everyone to work in the fields. This allowed some people to turn their attention to other pursuits like developing new technologies and social structures. Some of these advances (e.g., metallurgy) further enhanced the civilization's productivity as well as provided other advantages that enabled greater scale and sophistication. Over centuries the cumulative effect of this small difference in initial conditions gave Europeans a staggering advantage over the other societies they would encounter.

Further, Diamond notes that living in close proximity with domesticated animals over thousands of years increased Europeans' immunity to the diseases that these animals transmitted to humans. By contrast, other civilizations lacking this immunity were often decimated upon their first contact with

Europeans and with the diseases they carried.

Critics have labeled Diamond's work as "environmental determinism" – as placing too much emphasis on geographic factors as if the results could not have turned out differently. Diamond may unwittingly have invited this critique by subtitling his book, "The Fates of Human Societies." Critics of so-called "environmental determinism" may also resist Diamond's geographic focus since geography is difficult to change, and they have an emotional attachment to helping struggling societies improve their circumstances today.

At the same time, this criticism seems odd given that the alternative might be "biological determinism" – that is, attributing the disparate outcomes not to geography but to differences in innate human capacities. Diamond notes in his introduction his desire to explain societies' relative success without relying on biology (or on the social construct of race through which we often view biological differences).

We can change neither geography nor biology any time soon. But we can change institutions. Acemoglu and Robinson, referenced in Chapter 2 under the *structural* view, argue that institutions play the critical role in determining societal outcomes. They dismiss geographic factors, such as agricultural productivity and tropical diseases, entirely. Acemoglu and Robinson acknowledge that today's institutions reflect past choices, as in the case of two towns on the U.S.-Mexico border whose differences they trace to Spanish and English colonial practices. But at least there is hope. One can overcome these historical legacies and put in place the institutions that will lead to greater societal success – and less poverty – in the future.

Acemoglu and Robinson's resistance to Diamond's analysis of the subtle and long-term factors shaping societal success turns not on facts and evidence, but rather on their underlying way of thinking. Determinism – whether environmental, biological, or institutional – requires that the effect must be traceable to a manageable number of root causes, with other factors dismissed as largely irrelevant. Within this way of thinking, Acemoglu and Robinson select the solution that meets their emotional needs because they can implement it over a relatively short period of time, or at least within one's lifetime. (One cannot change geography that fast.) As John Kenneth Galbraith noted in Chapter 1, people often conceptualize the cause of poverty as the lack of whatever it is they seek to offer.

Few people would argue that having more productive plants and more useful animals yields *no* advantage to a nascent civilization.[11] What people find difficult, then, is the notion that plants and animals are the *most important* advantage, or in the case of Acemoglu and Robinson, that plants and animals trump the advantage that *they* think is most important – the presence of "inclusive institutions." However, if we allow for systems that are sensitive to initial conditions and to small perturbations along the way – more Plinko board than high school physics problem – then we can examine the role of geography without ruling out all the other things that may also be important.

The application of the Plinko board metaphor both to the success of entire countries and to the success of an individual within a country suggests that we are in a sense moving down many Plinko boards at the same time. We can conceptualize this in terms of another idea from chaos theory called self-similarity. Self-similarity describes how systems resemble themselves when observed at different scales. The geometric concept associated with self-similarity is the *fractal*, in which a geometric pattern is replicated on itself at smaller and smaller scales,

Figure 6.

producing a shape with infinite length within a finite area – the proverbial "world in a grain of sand."[12]

As an example, consider looking at a photo of a tree (see **Figure 6**). Without knowing the scale of the photo, you cannot tell if the photo shows the trunk, a limb, or a branch. The tree's structure looks the same (it is self-similar) when observed at any scale. These scales are "nested" together, meaning that one scale fits within the next.

Self-similarity across different scales – from civilization to country to community to individual, all of which operate as nonlinear systems (e.g., Plinko boards) – offers us an understanding of poverty (and of life) that completely confounds the Newtonian approach we have followed in the past. As humans, we live at the confluence of all these nonlinear dynamics working at multiple levels over the course of minutes, days, months, years, decades, generations, and millennia. We travel many Plinko boards simultaneously.

As individuals, we face situations in our own lives that push us one way or another on the board. As community members and as citizens, we participate in collective actions and reactions that shift the entire group. Some events of our lives may even have consequences for the future of the species. A single event can prove significant across multiple Plinko boards (e.g., the 9/11 attacks, a natural disaster), or it may only touch one person.

But the Plinko boards do not, on their own, explain our outcomes, since we are more than just the consequence of what happens around us. A human is different from a disc plodding its way down a Plinko board in that a human has choices. He or she can make these choices rationally or irrationally. Rationality allows a human to move with intentionality in the direction of his or her own choosing. But where does this rationality come from?

CHAPTER SEVEN

WHERE DOES RATIONALITY COME FROM?

"Which is better — to have rules and agree, or to hunt and kill?"

Piggy, in *Lord of the Flies*

No one is born rational or able to make decisions to care for oneself. Infants are completely dependent on others for their survival during the first few years of life, and even then, others take care of them until they reach an age when they can be sent out into the world to fend for themselves. At some point in this process, either before or after they leave home, some people achieve rationality in their thinking, while others do not. I am focusing on the notion of rationality for the reasons presented earlier, but let us keep in mind the other concepts to which it is related, such as competence and personal responsibility.

To understand rationality, we must look beyond economics and political science — the typical domains of the poverty discourse — to better understand what is occurring inside the individual. How does a person develop the capacity for thought and action that we would consider rational, particularly since *no one* has this capacity at birth?

Developmental psychologists study how people's capacities change over time, and over the past 100 years, they have provided a range of models to describe these processes. Jean Piaget began this work with children and described stages of cognitive development that still inform curriculum development in schools to this day. Other psychologists such as Abraham Maslow, Clare Graves, Erik Erikson, Lawrence Kohlberg, and Jane Loevinger extended their inquiries throughout the life course.

Loevinger sought to describe how one's "ego," or sense of identity (what the person refers to when saying the word "I"), developed over the course of the person's life. Based on many interviews, first with women and then with men, Loevinger proposed eight stages through which ego development occurs. While many such models describe essentially the same trajectory, albeit through different lenses, I will use Loevinger's model as the basis of this discussion since it is associated with a validated psychometric assessment: the Washington University Sentence Completion Test.[1] This assessment has already produced data relevant to our topic and could be used to test any hypotheses I propose.

Loevinger's developmental sequence passes through the following eight stages:

- Impulsive: Focused on "physical needs and impulses, dependent on others for control. There is little sense of causation. Rules are poorly understood."
- Self-Protective: Driven by "more or less

opportunistic hedonism; they lack long-term goals and ideals. They want immediate gratification and, if they can, will exploit others for their ends."

- Conformist: "Rules are accepted just because they are the rules ... There is a right way and a wrong way, and it is the same for everybody all the time, or at least for broad classes of people described in demographic terms."
- Self-Aware: "The person has become aware that not everyone, including his or her own self, conforms perfectly all the time to the characteristics that stereotypes seem to demand."
- Conscientious: "Recognition of multiple possibilities in situations leads to a sense of choice; decisions are made for reasons. The person strives for goals, tries to live up to ideals, and to improve the self."
- Individualistic: "There is a greater tolerance for individual differences ... Another new element is a concept of people as having and being different in different roles."
- Autonomous: "Recognition of other people's need for autonomy ... a deepened respect for other people and their need to find their own way and even make their own mistakes."
- Integrated: Since few people reach this stage, Loevinger relied on Abraham Maslow's description of the "self-actualizing person" in his well-known hierarchy of needs.[2]

Each stage repre-
sents a more complex
identity, much like a
set of Russian nesting
dolls that fit one within
the others. (See **Figure
7.**) When moving to the
next stage, a person de-
taches subjectively from

Figure 7.

what had previously been his or her conscious identity, and at-
taches to a larger identity that includes what came before. Some
of this identity is fundamentally new; Loevinger's criterion for
describing a new stage is that "it requires a new vocabulary to
describe it."[3] As Kegan and Lahey describe it, what had been
the "subject" of experience becomes an "object" experienced by
a more expansive "subject."[4]

For example, a toddler whose identity has been embedded in
momentary sensations of hunger, fatigue, agitation, or pleasure,
comes to see himself as an entity that persists through time and
can experience a sequence of different feelings, none of which
completely defines him. Similarly, a middle-aged woman who
has spent decades working toward individual goals discovers
that she is part of a community that includes many who have
been left behind. Through this process of expanding one's identity, a person discovers and develops new capacities to navigate
higher levels of complexity in the external world.

It is important to note a few common features of many such
developmental models. First, one passes through the stages in
sequence – that is, one cannot skip steps. Second, the pace at
which people move through these stages and the highest stage
they will reach vary from person to person.

A side-by-side comparison of attitudes and behaviors described in the sociological and psychological literature suggests that there may be some connection between ego development and socioeconomic status. As shown in **Figure 8**, the attitudes and behaviors associated with different social classes match those associated with different ego stages. Loevinger herself notes the similarity between her Impulsive stage and Lewis's "culture of poverty" construct.[5]

American Class Descriptions (Banfield, 57-63)	Ego Stage Descriptions (Hy and Loevinger, 4-7)
Upper — "places great value on ... 'developing one's potentialities to the full' ... is mindful of the rights of others and wants issues to be settled on their merits and by rational discussion, ... deplores bigotry."	**Integrated** — "Maslow's 'self-actualizing person.'" **Autonomous** — "recognition of other people's need for autonomy ... a deepened respect for other people and their need to find their own way and even make their own mistakes." **Individualistic** — "There is a greater tolerance for individual differences ... Another new element is a concept of people as having and being different in different roles."
Middle — "wants their children to go to college and to acquire the kind of formal training that will help them 'get ahead' ... has regard for the rights of others ... deplores bigotry and abhors violence [but] does not ... hold these attitudes as strongly as do members of the upper class."	**Conscientious** — "... recognition of multiple possibilities in situations leads to a sense of choice; decisions are made for reasons. The person strives for goals, tries to live up to ideals, and to improve the self." **Self-aware** — "The person has become aware that not everyone, including his or her own self, conforms perfectly all the time to the characteristics that stereotypes seem to demand."
Working — "emphasizes the virtues of neatness and cleanliness, honesty, obedience and respect for external authority ... it does not seem to occur to him that he is entitled to form opinions of his own ..."	**Conformist** — "Rules are accepted just because they are the rules ... There is a right way and a wrong way, and it is the same for everybody all the time, or at least for broad classes of people described in demographic terms."
Lower — "lives from moment to moment ... [sees the future as] something fixed, fated, beyond his control. Impulse governs his behavior ... [He] has a feeble, attenuated sense of self ... he is suspicious and hostile, aggressive yet dependent."	**Self-protective** — "... more or less opportunistic hedonism; they lack long-term goals and ideals. They want immediate gratification and, if they can, will exploit others for their ends." **Impulsive** — "... physical needs and impulses, dependent on others for control. There is little sense of causation. Rules are poorly understood."

Figure 8.

This suggests that people achieve the ability to take care of themselves in accordance with the most basic norms of their society in part by moving along a trajectory of psychological development. Before that point, however, *everyone* tends to express the earlier stages of ego development, which resemble the "culture of poverty." The "culture of poverty" is, in a sense, developmentally appropriate for anyone in the early stages of a normative developmental trajectory.

This accounts for researchers' frequent intimations of a link between the young and the poor. Loevinger herself commented that this link frustrated her efforts to develop the scoring protocols for the Washington University Sentence Completion Test:

> A problem in studying the lower stages by the means we chose, namely, reconstruction from adult and adolescent exemplars, was that the lower stage subjects tended to come from a different socioeconomic range than the median stage and high stage subjects. The obvious recourse was to study younger subjects from the same socioeconomic range as the college students and mothers' groups we began with. By the time we were committed to use of the SCT as our instrument of study, the use of young children became problematic [due to new restrictions on experimentation on children].[6]

Janet Castro notes the link between youth and lower-class behavior in a critique of the "culture of poverty" construct, writing:

So impressed was I by [research on "culturally deprived" lower-class children] that it did not occur to me to ask myself where in middle-class America was one going to find this abstractly intellectual bourgeois student interested only in self-expression, self-realization, and knowledge for its own sake?"[7]

Of course, such middle-class schoolchildren are rare if they exist at all, since the "culture of poverty" behaviors are developmentally appropriate for that age.

Ruby Payne shows the link between the "culture of poverty" and youth when she points out that middle-class people are more likely to fall into poverty behaviors earlier in life:

Adult personality is not considered to be formed until around age 29. From early adolescence until about that age, such factors as early pregnancy, drug/biochemical/addiction issues, learning disabilities, abuse, and social isolation (virtually no friends) can impact individuals and have them using the hidden rules of poverty, even though they may have been raised middle class.[8]

Oscar Lewis associates poverty behaviors with children, but because he views these behaviors as a cultural adaptation rather than as manifestations of early developmental stages, he asserts that their adoption renders poor children "psychologically unready to take full advantage of changing conditions or improving opportunities that may develop in their lifetime."[9] What Lewis misses is that at young ages virtually *all* children are in either the Impulsive or the Self-Protective stage, which map closely to the "culture of poverty" he describes. Perhaps these children have a greater potential to move to later ego stages than his "culture" construct allows.

Research comparing children and adults at these lower ego stages has identified differences in expression (e.g., the aggression of the Impulsive stage is more blatant in adults than in children), but the essential developmental priorities are the same.[10] The issue, then, is not that some people *enter* these stages (since we all do if we have any hope of developing further), but rather that some people do not *leave* these stages, or are delayed in doing so. Also of concern is the fact that during their time in these early stages some people may engage in unhealthy behaviors, such as unprotected sex and criminality, that limit their prospects later in life.

Empirical research supports the assertion that the poor tend to be in lower ego stages than the rich and middle class. For example, **Figure 9** summarizes the correlation between ego stage and socioeconomic class for a sample population in Curaçao in the Dutch Antilles, based on research by Harry Lasker using the Washington University Sentence Completion Test.[11]

Why the correlation? First, it makes sense that people would associate based on ego stage. People like to be with others who view the world in roughly the same terms that they do. Lower-stage simplicity bores them, and higher-stage complexity confounds them. This is why national elites prefer spending time with one another over spending time with the general population of their own countries.

Second, any community will socialize its members to the general attitudes and means of social interaction that already exist, which often correspond to particular ranges of ego stages.

**Distribution of Ego Stage
by Socio-Economic Status**

Ego Stage	Socio-Economic Status			
	Low	Middle	High	Total
Impulsive (I-2)	10.1%	4.6%	. . .	5.1%
	(8)	(7)		(15)
Self-Protective (Delta)	32.9	15.9	. . .	16.6
	(26)	(24)		(50)
Self-Protective/Conformist (Delta/3)	36.7	27.8	18.3	27.9
	(29)	(42)	(13)	(84)
Conformist (I-3)	12.7	27.2	23.9	22.6
	(10)	(41)	(17)	(68)
Self-Aware (I-3/4)	3.8	19.9	42.3	20.9
	(3)	(30)	(30)	(63)
Conscientious (I-4)	3.8	4.6	15.5	7.0
	(3)	(7)	(11)	(21)
Column Totals Percentage	26.2	50.2	23.6	100.0
Number of People	(79)	(151)	(71)	(301)

Figure 9.

The "distinct forms of social interaction" common within the community "may affect the probability of stage transition" among its members.[12]

Third, those who transition to the next ego stage may self-select into a community where social interactions reflect their new stage. We can see this in the case of someone raised in a rural village, a small town, or an inner-city neighborhood who "makes it out" to a more urban, cosmopolitan environment.

Fourth, to the extent that such individuals face structural barriers that prevent them from leaving, they will be unduly "trapped" in poverty conditions, and they may – as a practical matter – continue to exhibit the behaviors of the stage they have left behind. This would tend to reinforce the socializing tendencies mentioned above.

Of course, this correlation between ego stage and social class does not imply that all of those who reach a certain ego stage – e.g., the stage associated with rationality, which we will discuss later – will escape poverty. Some may encounter obstacles (disability, lack of jobs, racial or gender discrimination) that undermine their abilities to create better lives for themselves. Their paths down the Plinko board (as discussed earlier) just may not go where they would like to go. This mirrors Lewis's distinction between economic poverty (e.g., just not having enough money) and the "culture of poverty," only now with a psychological dimension.

Similarly, not everyone who is *not* poor has necessarily achieved the stage of psychological development associated with rationality. Inherited wealth or productive spouses can economically buffer some people at early ego stages. As a result, they likely enjoy a material standard of living beyond what they could sustain on their own. In fact, popular media consistently fixates on people with great financial resources who still manage to behave in self-destructive ways that are difficult to explain.

That said, people who have achieved rationality will be in a far better position psychologically to improve their own lives day-in and day-out as new opportunities arise, regardless of where they start. They will more likely recognize an opportunity and take consistent, effective steps to pursue it. They may be the people that Mead describes as able to overcome the challenges of their lives, or that Carson describes as having the "right mindset" – the people who, after you "take everything from them and put them on the street," will "be right back up there."[13]

But which stage of Loevinger's model corresponds to rationality?

∞

As seen in **Figure 10**, which again provides the core attributes of Loevinger's ego stages, at the Self-Protective stage people "lack long-term goals and ideals." The absence of a

Ego Stage Descriptions

Integrated — "Maslow's 'self-actualizing person.'"

Autonomous — "recognition of other people's need for autonomy ... a deepened respect for other people and their need to find their own way and even make their own mistakes."

Individualistic — "There is a greater tolerance for individual differences ... Another new element is a concept of people as having and being different in different roles."

Conscientious — "... recognition of multiple possibilities in situations leads to a sense of choice; decisions are made for reasons. The person strives for goals, tries to live up to ideals, and to improve the self."

Self-aware — "The person has become aware that not everyone, including his or her own self, conforms perfectly all the time to the characteristics that stereotypes seem to demand."

Conformist — "Rules are accepted just because they are the rules ... There is a right way and a wrong way, and it is the same for everybody all the time, or at least for broad classes of people described in demographic terms."

Self-protective — "... more or less opportunistic hedonism; they lack long-term goals and ideals. They want immediate gratification and, if they can, will exploit others for their ends."

Impulsive — "... physical needs and impulses, dependent on others for control. There is little sense of causation. Rules are poorly understood."

Figure 10.

long-term vision – of foresight – implies that this stage is not rational since we cannot distinguish behavior from impulse.[14]

At the Conformist stage, people believe "there is a right way and a wrong way, and it is the same for everybody all the time, or at least for broad classes of people described in demographic terms." As Loevinger notes, "Both the individual's adjustment and the possibility of a society depend on at least minimal capacity for conformity."[15] However, participation in society does not imply the ability to operate rationally within it, shaping the future rather than simply complying with society's expectations.

At the Self-Aware stage, a person will "become aware that not everyone, including his or her own self, conforms perfectly all the time to the characteristics that stereotypes seem to demand." This represents a loosening of the strictures of the Conformist stage, but still does not provide for rationality.

At the Conscientious stage, however, "recognition of multiple possibilities in situations leads to a sense of choice; decisions are made for reasons."[16] Making decisions for reasons rather than simply by impulse or social convention is the essence of rationality. "Reasons" implies a logic that connects causes in the past and present to effects in the future. The person can entertain alternative future outcomes and then take action to produce the outcomes they find most desirable.

Elsewhere, Loevinger says of the Conscientious stage that:

> The major elements of an adult conscience are present. They include long-term, self-evaluated goals and ideals, differentiated self-criticism, and a sense of responsibility ... The Conscientious person sees himself as the origin of his own destiny.[17]

From a developmental perspective, this is the ego stage at which one would, in most cases, expect the environment to bear the majority of the responsibility for any remaining poverty. The fundamental capacity of the individual is no longer the primary concern.

But there's a twist. Until now I have limited the discussion to rationality and I have left out concepts like personal responsibility or competence. I said earlier that while rationality refers to a cognitive process taking place within the individual, competence refers to the ability of a person to advance his or her own well-being.

On a theoretical level, rationality is a key component of competence. But on a practical level, a person can be competent without being rational. Let me explain.

Rationality assumes that we make decisions for reasons – that is, based on the relative benefits as compared to the costs. We expect a person at the Conscientious stage to make decisions that advance his or her well-being based on that logic.

Prior to this stage, people tend to conform to – or at least to obey – the norms of their communities. Remember that for someone at the Conformist stage, "rules are accepted just because they are the rules," and that someone at the Self-Protective stage can play by the rules (without internalizing them) in order to maximize one's own advantage (including the avoidance of punishment). At these stages, the social environment plays a larger role in whether or not the person's decisions advance their well-being, which is how I have defined competence.

Thus, people raised in the middle class get what we could call a "competence boost." As they play by the rules (Self-Protective) and then internalize the rules (Conformist), they are using middle-class rules that reflect the capacities of the

Conscientious stage, even if they themselves have not yet reached that stage. They do not have to; their forebears have done it for them, at least in aggregate, and have embedded this consciousness in what Ruby Payne calls the "hidden rules" of the middle class.

Whether or not the people could have come up with them on their own, these middle-class rules, which reflect the reasoned decision-making, goal orientation, and self-improvement of the Conscientious stage, provide a pathway for success in an urban, modern society. They ensure (in most cases) that the young person will meet the basic societal requirements in terms of education, employment, and sexual responsibility. In a sense, the "success sequence" identified by Haskins and Sawhill[18] is programmed into those who have grown up in the environment typically described as middle-class.

It never occurred to me as a child that I would *not* attend college. My parents had gone to college, and it was clear that they expected that my brother and I would too. I never made a reasoned decision to go to college based on the impact it would have on my future well-being as compared to the other available options. I'm not sure I even knew there *were* other options, and I am quite sure I did not know there was such a thing as the *future*.

I remember the moment, several years later, when I discovered that the future existed and that the decisions I had made in the past would affect what happened to me up ahead. (This may have been my first glimpse of the Conscientious stage.) I had finished my third year of college and I was relaxing with friends in Myrtle Beach, South Carolina, during the week between final exams and my university's graduation ceremony. Looking around at the graduating fourth-year students, I realized that one year hence I, too, would be graduating. Much to my chagrin, I *also* realized that two years earlier I had committed to spending four years in the U.S. Navy after graduation (in exchange for a Navy ROTC scholarship). What a realization! But as late as my awareness of the future came, I had never doubted that I would go to college (I was already more than halfway through) and that I would proceed into my own middle-class adulthood.

Obviously, many people do not grow up mindlessly conforming to rules that reflect a later ego stage than they themselves have achieved and that will likely point them to a middle-class life whether they intend it or not. Those who grow up in poverty may thereby face a disadvantage heretofore unacknowledged in the poverty literature – that is, that their egos must develop *further* than those of their middle-class peers. They must reach the Conscientious stage *on their own*. They cannot just rely on the developmental bequest of their forebears to guide their decisions.

Without this bequest, they may need to tap into a social environment other than their own family and community that reflects the values of the Conscientious stage. Of course, not having reached the Conscientious stage themselves, they will not do this explicitly because of its value for their future well-being. Perhaps they will make this connection only if the person on the other side of the relationship takes an interest in them. This may be what Ruby Payne describes as "bridging capital" – that is, relationships that help a person raised in poverty learn the "hidden rules" of the middle class. As an institution, the military often plays this role for young people who have grown up in poverty, as in the case of J.D. Vance[19] and of my own father. In particular, military basic training, or boot camp, may be one of the most underappreciated anti-poverty interventions in the U.S.

Put simply, those raised in the middle class can become competent (that is, able to advance their own well-being) without being rational just by doing what their parents and teachers tell them to do. Those raised in poverty – absent a significant middle-class mentor – must attain rationality (that is, the Conscientious stage) on their own to achieve that same ability.

This explains Loevinger's reluctance to map her own model to Lewis's "culture of poverty" despite the obvious similarities. As she writes:

> The sketch of the Impulsive character type has much in common with Lewis's description of the "culture of poverty," but that surely is within the range of normal.[20]

The reference to "the range of normal" may reflect the notion that even those moving along a normative trajectory of ego development may exhibit traits consistent with the Impulsive – or, I would add, the Self-Protective – stage without themselves occupying these stages in a psychological sense. In aggregate, the psychological becomes sociological.

This implies an inherent inequity in the notion expressed earlier by David Ellwood, Ron Haskins, and Isabel Sawhill that social policy should focus on helping those who demonstrate rationality, competence, and personal responsibility. Such policies essentially "grandfather" middle-class youth into the middle class (figuratively and literally), while poor youth need to make it in on their own.

CHAPTER EIGHT

PUTTING IT ALL TOGETHER

"The rule of thumb is that the complexity of the organism has to match the complexity of the environment at all scales in order to increase the likelihood of survival."

Yaneer Bar-Yam

Our discovery in Chapter 6 that small differences in initial conditions can produce large differences in outcomes allows us to reframe the way the environment contributes to poverty. We realize that the metaphor of a high school physics problem, in which a ball must somehow cross an arbitrary "poverty line" by moving along a linear surface, but may be inhibited by traps, barriers, and forces, does not yield a sufficiently complex understanding, and that the metaphor of the Plinko board serves us much better. This allows us to account for the disproportionate impact of Ben Carson's mother, as well as the disproportionate impact of the desirable plant and animal species available to the early civilizations of the Fertile Crescent.

Similarly, the link between ego development and socioeconomic class allows us to reframe the notion of a "culture of poverty." Typically, we view this culture as an "adaptation" or an "accommodation" to the circumstances of poverty. This view assumes that the poor were previously in a preadaptation state in which they exhibited mainstream attitudes and behaviors (and perhaps were not poor). In most cases, this seems very unlikely.

The correlation between socioeconomic class and the trajectory of ego development suggests that *all* humans started out in the early ego stages. It is the humans who have moved *beyond* those stages who have done something different, who have "adapted" or "accommodated" to their environment.

Lewis unknowingly offers a natural experiment for determining which one of these explanations is correct. He states that the "culture of poverty" emerges under certain conditions, namely a cash economy with wage labor and high unemployment, a lack of organizing mechanisms for the poor, a bilateral kinship system,[1] and a societal narrative that values upward mobility and material success.[2]

However, Lewis also notes that:

> Where slums are isolated from their surroundings by enclosing walls or other physical barriers, where rents are low and residence is stable and where the population constitutes a distinct ethnic, racial or language group, the sense of community may approach that of a village.[3]

This is a fascinating statement. Lewis describes a distinct cultural pattern and asserts that this pattern *emerges* within a cash economy with wage labor and other specific features. He then notes that when communities exhibiting this pattern are sufficiently isolated from those features, they behave much like a village – that is, much like how virtually all pre-industrial societies behaved.

This suggests that the people in this community did not *adapt* to their poverty; rather, their poverty (and the associated isolation from the broader society) is the consequence of their *not having adapted* to new structures enacted by their society. It could also be due to their new arrival in that society, having moved from less complex environments. The "culture of poverty" does not *emerge* under the conditions listed by Lewis; rather, it *becomes visible* through its contrast with emerging social structures and with the emerging mental complexity they imply.

This explains why the "culture of poverty" is most often observed among migrant populations coming from the countryside – what Michael Harrington calls "urban hillbillies" in the U.S. context. They persist in the behaviors that served them well in rural life, but "the backwoods has completely unfitted them for urban life."[4]

With respect to immigrants, Lawrence Mead notes:

> The most successful groups in economic terms [in the U.S.] have been those (such as Jews and Asians) that were already urbanized in their countries of origin, committed to remaining in America, and hardworking in school and on the job ... The least successful groups, at least initially, were those who came from rural or peasant backgrounds, sometimes came only for the short term, and were less diligent as workers.[5]

Migrants from less complex environments may themselves adopt new attitudes and behaviors to navigate urban life, or (more typically) they may leave this task to their children or grandchildren. In either case, the fundamental capacity of such groups to adapt to their more complex new homes, either over time or across generations, explains Mead's qualification of "at least initially." As Banfield points out, most if not all ethnic groups within the U.S. have climbed the multigenerational ladder to socioeconomic integration in American society.[6]

The most reasonable conclusion, then, is not that the "culture of poverty" reflects an adaptation to poverty by communities that previously exhibited more recognizable attitudes and behaviors (by today's middle-class standards), but rather that *all* human societies started their journeys in the lower ego stages, and that humans have, to varying degrees, constructed and adapted to more complex environments ever since. Since poverty is the initial condition of the human species, then the "culture of poverty" is likely its initial culture.

So, what happened?

The variation in ego development started long ago, with some people moving to higher stages. We have no way of knowing what the distribution might have been in an early human society.

Those at higher stages gained more power within their societies (e.g., as chiefs or priests) since they were able to solve more complex problems. With their power, they created new social structures that reflected the higher levels of complexity they had attained. As noted earlier, Loevinger's criterion for defining a new ego stage is that "it requires a new vocabulary to describe it."[7] This may be true for social institutions as well as for language: the institutional vocabulary of the lower stages (e.g., tribes, clans) was insufficient to materialize the social aspirations of those with an expanded mental complexity.

As these new social structures appeared, those at lower ego stages needed to shift upward to the stages that allowed them to participate in – though not necessarily to lead – these structures. Consistent with this idea, Jared Diamond points out that a critical difference between rich and poor societies today is the length of time spent under a centralized government. While centralized governments emerged in Europe around 4,000 years ago, they appeared in sub-Saharan Africa within the last millennium or two.[8] Adapting to new social structures takes time.

Within any society, some made this shift, and some did not. Many who did not likely lived at some distance from the new structures (e.g., in the countryside) and could thus continue living much as they always had. Those who lived in close proximity to the new structures but found them overwhelming (in a psychological sense) likely formed smaller communities (e.g., slums, ghettos) that kept their distance. It is also important to note that those creating the new structures often embedded within them a privileged position for themselves and did not wholly welcome other groups.

This sounds like a pretty complex process, but let's take it one step further. Imagine that this co-evolution between humans and the social structures they are creating is taking place as individuals, communities, societies, and the species move down multiple Plinko boards at the same time, subject to small differences (e.g., the availability of more productive plant species[9]) and random chance (e.g., the defeat of the Spanish Armada[10]). Not only that, but they are also interacting with one another as they go. In some cases, these interactions are nudges, such as when societies engage in trade or intellectual exchange. In other cases, they are disruptive or even catastrophic for one or both parties, as in the case of war, colonization, or enslavement. This is how we got the world we have today.

In this framing, poverty takes on a new definition. As Yaneer Bar-Yam notes in the quote that begins this chapter, an organism's likelihood of survival (and by extension, a human's likelihood of functioning effectively in society) is a function of how well it matches the complexity of the environment in which it lives. Poverty, then, is an emergent property of a system in which some members of the population lack the complexity required to engage effectively with the critical structures of that environment.

This framing belies the notion that we will ever "eradicate poverty." Societies will continue to increase in complexity, and there will always be those whose own complexity has fallen behind. We will just adjust and expand our objective definition of poverty, as we have many times before. (Referring back to the emotional definition of poverty in Chapter 1, we will reset the poverty threshold to the level of material lack that produces a significant emotional response in the context of the times.)

Figure 11 shows a meager attempt to display this framing of poverty graphically. In order to represent the benefits of higher ego stages for moving to the right on the Plinko board, I have inverted the sequence of the Russian nesting dolls – that is, the larger dolls now represent the lower ego stages, and the smaller dolls represent the higher stages. Because the gaps between the pegs get narrower as you move to the right on the board, only those at the higher stages are likely to make it through. It is a cumbersome depiction, but at the very least it should show the inadequacy of a simple ball sitting on a linear surface!

This way of thinking about poverty incorporates the best

PLINKO

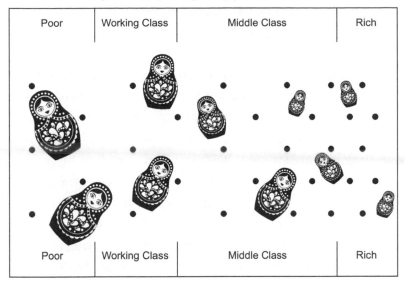

Poor	Working Class	Middle Class	Rich

Poor	Working Class	Middle Class	Rich

Figure 11.

aspects of each quadrant while leaving behind the aspects by which each quadrant falls short:

- It incorporates the "personal responsibility" of the *behavioral* view without holding the poor to an arbitrary standard that some may never meet.
- It incorporates the "culture of poverty" of the *cultural* view, but with a developmental reframing that allows people to move beyond this "culture" on their own as they move through life.
- It incorporates the *structural* view by recognizing society's ability to alter the context (the Plinko board) for better or for worse, but it does not ignore human agency altogether.

- It incorporates the *contextual* view in that it acknowledges the need to set the context for good decisions for all of us, but it does not overreach by assuming *a priori* that the poor are just as rational as the middle class.

What kinds of action does this new way of thinking suggest? I will offer initial thoughts related to domestic poverty in the U.S., and leave global poverty to a future book or discussion.

First, the inherent uncertainty of the Plinko board and the notion that some Americans lack the ability to take care of themselves – through no fault of their own – point to the value of putting in place stronger basic supports for all to enjoy. These could include, for example, a basic guaranteed income and universal health insurance. Currently, society views these as highly politicized issues, yet they need not be. Both would satisfy important concerns of all four perspectives: the *behavioral* view's disdain for employment disincentives associated with receiving federal benefits, the *structural* view's concern about income inequality, the *contextual* view's desire to reduce the stresses of poverty, and the herein-reframed *cultural* view's recognition that not everyone can take care of himself or herself.

Second, there is an opportunity to embed the *behavioral* view's "success sequence" (finish high school, get a job, and marry before having children) in the Plinko board itself. For example, Sawhill proposes expanding access to long-acting reversible contraception (LARC), such as implants and intra-uterine devices (IUDs).[11] As much as we might like our daughters to abstain from sex until they are emotionally ready, the developmental perspective makes clear that in most cases the rationality necessary to prevent an unplanned pregnancy does not emerge until an ego stage that most people do not reach until after their teen years, if not later. Thus, providing IUDs free of charge to any woman who wanted one would essentially take unplanned pregnancy (and many abortions as well) off the table – or rather, off the Plinko board. We could embed other aspects of the "success sequence" through compulsory education to age eighteen or a universal youth employment program (think boot camp for civilians) to instill basic job skills and work habits following high school graduation.

Third, we can actively apply the developmental perspective to craft a society that supports the healthy development of each of its members. This is already happening in communities that have this sensibility. For example, social service agencies are shifting from a "case management" model to a "coaching" model. Schools are adopting a "whole child" approach or teaching social and emotional learning (SEL). The nonprofit Circles USA[12] creates support groups for the poor that include members of the middle class who can offer both links to new opportunities and what Ruby Payne calls "bridging capital."

Fourth, we can review our current policies through a developmental lens to make sure we are not exploiting those at lower ego stages. For example, many states have expanded state-sanctioned gambling, including both casinos and state lotteries, justifying such efforts with the logic that gambling is a choice – those who do it must derive value (e.g., fun) from it. Those at lower ego stages, who hold superstitious beliefs and are unable to envision a range of futures that might follow from the actions they take today, are more likely to participate in gambling activities than those at higher stages. In this sense, we can see state-sanctioned gambling as a "developmental tax" that disproportionately collects revenues from those at lower ego stages. It is striking how many elected leaders decry the bad behavior of the poor when it *costs* money (e.g., through welfare programs) yet welcome the bad behavior of the poor when it *raises* money (e.g., through state-sanctioned gambling).

Fifth, we can learn more effectively about poverty. Complexity theory has provided the tool of agent-based modeling. Unlike traditional models, which apply a certain set of programmed probabilities to a given set of inputs, agent-based models populate a certain environment with any number of autonomous entities ("agents") governed by their own probabilities. As these agents interact within the environment, they can produce results never envisioned by the modeler. For example, a sufficiently complex model of political activity in a democracy might, under certain conditions, yield results as surprising as a revolution or a dictatorship.

Imagine an agent-based model in which we can test our poverty interventions in virtual space before implementing them in the real world. The modeled environment would have all the uncertainty of a Plinko board, while we would assign agents to different developmental stages (e.g., of Loevinger's model). By matching the agents to a real-life population according to the proportion in each stage, one could model the impact of various poverty interventions. Further, by modeling different contexts, one could investigate why an intervention worked in one context but not in another. It would change the research question from "what works?" to "what works where and when, and why?"

Now imagine converting this agent-based model into a video game that anyone can play. Game designer Jane McGonigal has argued that to solve today's problems we need to increase the amount of time we spend playing video games. A game version of the agent-based model described above might elicit – and evaluate – a range of poverty innovations never seen before.

These are initial thoughts on the opportunities that emerge from the way of thinking about poverty presented in this chapter. Hopefully, this has prompted new ideas for you as well. But beyond changing what we might do, this way of thinking about poverty offers the chance to change who we are – to meet the *adaptive* challenge of poverty mentioned in the introduction.

This way of thinking helps us release the negative emotions we have felt about poverty – and that have locked us in limited understandings – because it adheres to the premises identified at the end of Chapter 4 – those realities that our emotions help us to avoid: the randomness, uncertainty, regretfulness, and finitude of life; the chance we will have no impact at all; the necessity of growth through struggle.

We can now establish new principles for what we might do and identify new emotions we might feel, thereby becoming more potent change agents in the world. This will be the topic of the final chapter.

CHAPTER NINE

PRINCIPLES AND EMOTIONS

"I have hopes that the past will be found to have been all right for what it was. And the present, this present of ours, I hope will be found to have been all right for what it was."

Robert Frost

One has to marvel at how far humans have come. What started as a miserable ordeal has blossomed into the richness of a global society that has pulled 6.4 billion people out of poverty by today's definition, and that's just counting those who are alive right now.[1]

But clearly, that is not the whole story. There remains unspeakable suffering in the world, and it is natural to want to reduce it, and to accelerate as much as we can the progress that has been underway for so many years.

In Chapter 1, I defined poverty in terms of the emotional response evoked in an observer. Some readers may have interpreted that definition as implying that poverty is not a big deal in its own right. In fact, what that definition tells me is that poverty *is* a big deal, and always will be.

There will always be people whose material wants evoke an emotional response in others, even if those wants are significantly less severe than they are today. As British researcher Jonathan Tanner notes, "To see a world in which so many people have less than you and to want them to have more is, to many of us, human nature."[2]

For this reason, I find talk about "eradicating poverty" to be confusing. If we ever eradicated poverty as multilateral organizations define it today, I suspect we would just redefine it at a higher threshold and start eradicating it all over again. That's human nature: We always want to improve the lives of those who have less than we do. There is no finish line.

So how might the understanding of poverty outlined in the previous chapter guide our efforts to do so? Several principles come to mind. By observing these principles and by wrestling in each case with how best to apply them, we can take action to reduce poverty without falling into the conflicts and inconsistencies brought about by a more limited understanding.

Principle 1: The first principle comes from our incorporation of developmental psychology into the poverty discourse. Terri O'Fallon expresses this principle as a "developmental right" – that is, that every individual has "the right to be developmentally at whatever stage one occupies."[3] There is no "good" or "bad" within the Loevinger stages of ego development that I have been using in this book, or in any of the other models to which it maps. An adult is not *better* than a child; the adult (assuming normative development) is just able to handle more complex situations more effectively and with less stress.

Similarly, there is nothing *wrong* with a poor person who operates at the Impulsive, Self-Protective, or any other ego stage of Loevinger's model. Without the broader awareness that would come from having experienced higher ego stages, they cannot even recognize the limitations of their worldview and their sense of identity. A fish in water does not know it is in water; it has never known anything else.

We understand this when we deal with our own children; we translate more complex concepts into simple terms they can readily understand. But when interacting with other adults we often assume a level of mental complexity that they may not actually possess.

This is why David Ellwood's suggestion that we need a social system where "everyone who exercises reasonable responsibility can make it without welfare"[4] is incomplete (and potentially inhumane). That standard may work for those in poverty who have reached a point in their own psychological development where they can take responsibility for themselves – that is, where they can make and implement plans to improve their own lives. (In Chapter 7, I mapped this to the Conscientious stage – at least for those not raised in a middle-class environment.)

But to apply this standard to everyone would set up many of the poor to fail. Society can only expect of a citizen what that citizen can accomplish; otherwise, the expectation is just a premeditated resentment. The poor become outcasts in their own land.

It would be great if those at earlier ego stages could jump to the stages where they could work consistently toward goals that would improve their own lives. Unfortunately, a person cannot skip steps along the sequence of ego stages. This means that O'Fallon's developmental right has a longitudinal dimension: all persons have the right not only to be where they are right now, but to follow the developmental trajectory they are on – to live their own journey one step at a time.

Without this developmental awareness, governments and donors often expect the poor to jump up several stages because they project their own ego stage onto the poor. Those at the Conformist and Self-Aware stages will expect the poor to sign on to a set of dogmatic norms, as in the case of faith-based charities that require religious commitment as a precondition for assistance. Those at the Conscientious stage will prioritize individual achievement and material success through entrepreneurship and economic liberalization. Those at the Individualistic stage will demand tolerance and social inclusion. But these advancements may require psychological capacities beyond what some can access.

This may explain, for example, Banerjee and Duflo's finding that, despite all the excitement of Western donors for the entrepreneurs among the poor, what these so-called entrepreneurs wanted most for their children is that they should get a government job.[5] The next step up from Self-Protective is Conformist; the next step up from peddling goods for survival is the stability of a monthly paycheck from a system in which you know your place.

I wonder if the same thing may now be happening in the U.S. health equity movement. Health equity refers to "the absence of avoidable, unfair, or remediable differences [in health] among groups of people, whether those groups are defined socially, economically, demographically or geographically or by other means of stratification."[6]

The health equity movement in the U.S. has appropriately expanded the discourse on health to include non-medical factors like housing, transportation, education, and employment (the so-called "social determinants of health"[7]) that play a far greater role in shaping health outcomes than medical care itself. The resulting systemic understanding of health is impressive – so impressive, in fact, that it may exceed the mental capacity of many in the poor communities that some philanthropies and nonprofits now seek to organize as advocates for health equity.

While noble in theory, I believe that such efforts may unwittingly project onto poor communities the mental complexity required to grasp the multidimensional concept of health equity. People at lower ego stages may use the term "health equity," but as in the case of entrepreneurship above, it may mean very different things, and the disparity may go undetected until something goes wrong (e.g., failed investments, broken commitments).

The term "health equity" seems to reflect the "greater tolerance for individual differences" and the holistic thinking of Loevinger's Individualistic stage. By introducing this construct as the basis for engaging people in poor communities, many of whom are unlikely to have reached this stage, the leaders of the health equity movement may actually embed inequity in the conversation by using terms beyond the grasp of many they seek to engage. Rather than propagating a construct that many cannot fully access, a better approach might be to *practice* health equity – that is, simply to meet people where they are, to engage them in a conversation about their most urgent needs, and to work across multiple factors to expand the possibility for them to become the best next version of themselves, whatever that may be.

Of course, when people do become the best next version of themselves (in developmental terms), the resulting behaviors often strike governments and donors as undesirable or worse. For example, those at the Impulsive stage survive through an orientation of submission to and dependence on the powers-that-be around them. A shift to the Self-Protective stage, then, might be indicated by manipulation and opportunism to maximize one's short-term self-interest. This might show up as gang activity within rich countries[8] or as government corruption in poor countries.

A shift onward to the Conformist stage might show up as the adoption of a fierce "us versus them" bigotry framed in national, racial, ethnic, or religious terms. As psychologist Erik Erikson writes, "Tribal, national, and class identity [in normative development] ... demand that man consider otherness inimical."[9] Similarly, movement to the Conscientious stage may appear as self-serving material enrichment – the "elite capture" for which social activists often criticize a country's business or political elite. Human development is a messy business, and progress does not always look like progress as it happens.

If everyone has the right to be at whatever level he or she is at, then that means *everyone*. Not just the poor, but all of us. That means that we must come to terms with behaviors we initially find disconcerting. The corrupt local official in the hinterland of a poor country, the domineering husband who believes a woman's place is in the home, the bigot, the CEO who pays himself several hundred times his company's median salary – all these may be expressing developmental urges that are appropriate for the stages they occupy within Loevinger's model.

Coming to terms with these behaviors does not mean that we necessarily allow them to continue. It does, however, mean that we must be more thoughtful in how we address them. Shaming the people for whom these behaviors are developmentally appropriate is unlikely to lead to progress. If we shame successfully, the person may regress to the previous stage, which offers a reduced capacity for addressing the challenges they experience in life. If our shaming fails, they may dig in around their behaviors (now in secrecy) and become fierce opponents of social change. As mediator Marshall Rosenberg writes, "It is a rare human being who can maintain focus on our needs when we are expressing them through images of their wrongness."[10]

The invitation here is not to tolerate all behavior that can be considered developmentally appropriate, but rather to take a broader perspective on the behaviors that anti-poverty activists often resist so vigorously. Also, to recognize that even those behaviors that seem most contrary to human progress may in some situations represent precisely the human progress those activists seek to bring about. We are all on our own journeys and have the right to make our own mistakes.

Principle 2: Speaking of mistakes, the second principle is that everyone has the right to the consequences of his or her own actions. Humans co-evolved with our environment over many thousands of years only through much trial and error. Whenever we humans take an action (be it a toddler taking her first step or a nation launching a new policy) and experience its consequences, we receive important feedback that helps us grow. Without those consequences, we may survive in the short term, but we may miss out on growth that could serve us well in the future.

Some consequences are built into life itself. If a woman has unprotected sex, then there is a certain probability that she will become pregnant. That is just how biology works.

The various pathways open to her *after* she becomes pregnant are subject to our decisions as a society. Imagine that the pregnant woman is unmarried. What consequences will she face? Will she be tried for a crime, shunned, or even killed? Will she be allowed to terminate the pregnancy? Will she be eligible for government assistance? Can she demand child support from the baby's father? These are all consequences that various societies have put in place for this situation.

Thus, collectively we shape the consequences that each of us experiences when we take certain actions. We do this by adding or removing pegs, ramps, and barriers on the Plinko board(s) along which we all travel. In the process, we must distinguish between consequences that promote growth and learning, and consequences that simply punish. But how do we know which is which?

We humans tend to hold two values with respect to consequences: justice and mercy. Justice here means, quite simply, that a person must face the logical consequences of actions, or as they say in law enforcement, "If you do the crime, you do the time [in prison]." Mercy we associate with letting people off the hook, or making an exception based either on extenuating circumstances or on our own unilateral beneficence.

As we shape the Plinko board, we need to connect justice and mercy in a new way. I propose that true justice can only exist *within* mercy – within a genuine concern for the person's well-being.[11] Justice without mercy is indistinguishable from cruelty and punishment. When mercy is present, however, negative consequences serve not only to deter others but also to guide the person toward better actions in the future.

My first publication on poverty was an article called "What if we loved the poor?"[12] in which I compared the challenge of reducing poverty to the challenge of raising a child. In both cases, we must figure out how to care for others who are fundamentally dependent on us for the time being, but who we hope will one day be able to take care of themselves. Both require us to guide a person (or people) through a sequential process of individual development in a bewilderingly complex context.

I continue to believe that this is the appropriate lens for calibrating the consequences we, as members of a society (or species), create for each other. Specifically, would we consider a certain consequence to be just if it fell upon our own child, or upon someone else we love?

I also believe that this is the appropriate lens for viewing those who behave in ways we find disturbing, such as the corrupt local official, the domineering husband, the bigot, and the overpaid CEO we mentioned earlier. Imagine that one of those people is your own cousin. What consequences would you consider appropriate for the person's actions? Perhaps we could reprimand or fire the local official. We could challenge the husband in his beliefs and offer his wife tools for negotiating with him while preserving the marriage. We could invite the bigot into meaningful conversation with people from the groups he claims to disdain. We could subject the CEO's salary to external evaluation and require him to return the excessive compensation from previous years.

As a society, we can impose consequences on people's actions; the right to be where they are does not imply the right to act however they wish. But we must do so from the perspective of concern for their well-being as well as for our own. Otherwise, we violate their "developmental right" by making them into an enemy simply for exhibiting behaviors that are appropriate for where they are at the time. This creates more conflict in the world, rather than less, and it likely slows their development at the same time.

In Chapter 3, I quoted Martin Luther King Jr.'s statement that "noncooperation with evil is as much a moral obligation

174 | REFRAMING POVERTY

as is cooperation with good." Notably, King's reasoning was not that one might be sullied by the evil inflicted by others, but rather that such acquiescence "is a way of allowing [the oppressor's] conscience to fall asleep. At this moment the oppressed fails to be his brother's keeper."[13] We condemn evil not to shame or punish those who do it, but rather to express our genuine concern for their well-being as well as ours, and to help them move beyond it.

Principle 3: The third principle is that everyone is worthy of a healthy and fulfilling life, whether or not that actually happens. Some readers may wonder why I have expressed this just as a principle and not as a right. If everyone is worthy of it, then why shouldn't everyone have it?

They should. But it does not make sense to assert a right that we cannot currently assure and enforce. To do so would simply evoke new anger that would spin itself into new conflicts and new stories of who is to blame that the right has gone unfulfilled. (See Part One!) No one is to blame. Humans just do not – for now, anyway – have the ability to assure everyone a healthy and fulfilling life. Even if we have the necessary material resources, the required sensibilities to distribute those resources equitably are still in short supply.

As unpleasant as it may seem, this is the fundamental tension in which we humans live – in the space between what we are and what we can be, between how far we have come and how far we wish to go, between human reality and human aspiration. Every day we feel the temptation to collapse this tension – either to give up hope that things might ever get better or to conclude that we have found the answer (if only people would listen to us!). The difficulty of being human is to live in the tension – to live by our principles and to do what we believe is right in each moment, recognizing all the while that we will never fully resolve the tension.

We do not like this one bit! We look out upon a suffering world and scream, "Make it stop!" We want so desperately for the world to be other than the way it is. This aversion to our current reality reflects much of what is good about us humans – our empathy, our compassion, and our desire not to see others suffer. But it also leads us toward limited understandings as a means for keeping at bay the negative emotions generated by living in a world that is less than we would like it to be.

The alternative is to accept the world exactly as it is. This does not preclude us from wanting to change it, but we do recognize that it is the way it is right now. This simple step gives us a foothold from which to begin our efforts in earnest. Further, it immediately converts our emotions from existential avoidance maneuvers (à la Sartre) to sources of invaluable insight.

Even after we have accepted the world as it is, we will continue to feel things like guilt, anger, disgust, etc. The difference will be that the emotions will not turn into moods; they will not bind us to limited understandings of reality that both justify and protect us from how we feel inside. We will be able to – and will *have* to – let them wash over us and hear the messages they carry. We will then be able to apply those messages in our lives and in our work.

Empathic healer Karla McLaren details how much we can learn from our emotions if we listen to what they want to tell us.[14] Emotions ask us important questions that focus our attention on the work we must do. Anger asks, "What must be protected? What must be restored?" Shame asks, "Who has been hurt? What must be made right?" Contempt asks, "What [part of me] has fallen into my shadow? What must be reintegrated?"

If we welcome our emotions and explore the questions they ask of us, we reset our boundaries, we correct our own behavior, we accept ourselves more completely, and we do the other work necessary to make our lives more fulfilling and to better equip us to serve the world.

The hardest work is to discern between the messages for us and the messages for the world. We must figure out if the need for work suggested by our emotions genuinely exists in the world or if it belongs to our own life and story. In most cases, it is both, but we must handle each part of it in the domain where it belongs. As a good friend of mine says, "You have to check the tags on the bags." Or as McLaren writes:

> If we try to right wrongs, end injustice, and save
> the world before we've become integrated and
> upright, we tend to drag our unconscious shad-
> ow material [the parts of ourselves that we have
> rejected] right into the heart of our crusades.[15]

Fortunately, when we accept the world, an individual emotion like anger or guilt does not turn into a mood that persists independent of events, creating conflict within us, with others, and with the poor. This frees up space in our consciousness for other emotions not typically associated with poverty that can fuel and motivate us in new ways.

One of these is joy. What a privilege it is to be able to serve one's fellow human beings and to alleviate their suffering. What a joy it is to give one's unique gifts to a world in so much need. So many people say they are *passionate* about helping the poor; they may not know that the Latin root of the word "passion" is *pati*, to suffer. By contrast, those who are *joyful* in their work experience a feeling of fulfillment in doing the work itself rather than only in achieving the impact one has in mind.

Another is longing, which means craving or desiring, but for something distant or unattainable. Longing is the emotion of living knowingly in the tension between reality and aspiration, the emotion of the traveler reminiscing of home but realizing that she still has business to conduct abroad. Longing is one-part fervent desire and one-part melancholy – an aching sense of living in what must be, at least for now. It reminds the heart of the preciousness of every moment and of the valor of every attempt.

Faith comes from the Latin *fidere*, "to trust," and refers here not to religious belief but to a deeply held confidence in the future. One who is faithful is in relationship with something – oneself, another person, God, or the universe. This relationship keeps one moving forward even when times are tough.

And let us not forget awe. Awe is what we feel when we recognize that we are part of something much greater than ourselves. Each of us is a participant on a journey that is at least 200,000 years in the making, and that could continue – through various twists and turns – for many years to come. Awe would seem to offer great comfort to all those who feel the intense burden of their poverty work. Awe invites us to participate, but also to be patient, reminding us that the work is not ours alone to do.

EPILOGUE

"Truth is a pathless land."

J. Krishnamurti

I believe there are two fundamental spiritual truths. The first is that we are all connected. The second is that each of us is completely alone.

The first of these probably seems obvious to those engaged in anti-poverty work. As the African concept of *ubuntu* is often translated, "I am because we are." It is this sense of mutuality at the community and global levels that leads many people to work to reduce the suffering of those around them.

At the same time, we each experience the world from our own unique points of consciousness; we must take it on faith that anyone or anything else exists at all. For all we know, the entire universe has been created for our own learning and growth. Given the frequency with which situations requiring us to grow appear in our lives, that seems like a reasonable conclusion. As

Jewish rabbi Abraham Joshua Heschel writes, "It is as if I were the only man on the globe and God, too, were alone, waiting for me."[1]

As humans, we must make a separate peace with each of these realities – with our membership in a global community and with our solitary existence. What exists between the two is not so much a boundary as it is a wormhole connecting two different yet parallel universes. Issues in one universe show up in corresponding forms in the other. And we must discover for ourselves what right living, for us, looks like in each.

When we do so, and when we achieve a harmony between the two, we attain Erikson's definition of wisdom as "detached concern with life itself, in the face of death itself."[2] The detachment comes from the awareness of our solitude, and of our limited abilities to shape the future even for ourselves, let alone for distant generations to come. The concern comes from our deep connections to everyone and everything else, from the awareness that we are all just swirls in one global movement that has been and will be for a long time to come. Together, this wisdom creates a powerful place from which to improve the world, with no attachment to its improvement.

I have always been comfortable with this detachment. My mother remembers a time when I was around ten years old when she asked if I was worried about something that was not going particularly well in my life, and I replied, "I figure that if it won't matter in twenty years, then it probably doesn't matter that much right now."

As a futurist, I have continued to hold a long-term perspective, not minding that the moral arc of the universe is long.[3] My job has been to help people find their places on that arc, whether they will see it bend in their lifetimes or not. Similarly, as a teacher of social enterprise, I have prodded my students' thinking in new directions largely because I am not directly involved in the sort of immediate work they hope to do.

I hope that this book has put my detachment in the service of your concern – that it has prompted you to think and feel differently, to re-examine your current perspectives, and to find better ways of doing the work you do. Detachment does not mean not caring. Rather, it protects one's caring from the slide into projection, attachment, misunderstanding, and conflict. I hope that these ideas help you along your own journey toward the wisdom of detached concern, since I believe there is no more powerful place from which to work.

∽

One evening as I was working on this book in Kramerbooks & Afterwords, a restaurant and bookstore in Washington, D.C., a woman at the table next to me made the comment, "If we knew how to eradicate poverty, we would have done it already." I find that comment surprising, yet I suspect it reflects a common misconception wrought by a failure – or an unwillingness – to live in the inherent and essential tension of human life.

We do know how to eradicate poverty. We have been doing it for 200,000 years. We have brought the poverty rate down from 100.0 percent to a mere 10.7 percent, and most of that decrease has occurred during the last 200 years. During the same period, we have increased global life expectancy from twenty-nine to over seventy years,[4] the five-year survival rate from 57.3 percent to 92.7 percent,[5] and adult literacy rates from 10 to over 80 percent.[6] We know exactly what we're doing!

Remarkably, most of these gains have not come from the

work of NGOs, nonprofits, or even government agencies focused on poverty reduction. Rather, they have come from everyday humans trying to improve their own lives, year after year, century after century, millennium after millennium.

Notably, even the widely heralded achievement of the first Millennium Development Goal – to halve poverty between 1990 and 2015 – resulted not from explicit efforts to reduce poverty but rather from global economic growth, particularly in countries like China and Indonesia that have consistently eschewed the recommendations of global organizations. Truth be told, formal efforts to reduce poverty are a sideshow when compared to the organic pursuit of self-improvement and self-actualization in which we humans have been engaged since the dawn of time.

One of the biggest forces for poverty reduction has been the nudges we give each other as we make our way down the Plinko board. Ben Carson's mother. My father's high school English teacher. A traveler passing through a Chinese mountain village, mentioning to my wife's parents a newly opened "prodigy class" at a boarding school in the city. Neighbors and friends who have pointed J.D. Vance and many more like him on to a better life.

What the Plinko board makes visible is that poverty reduction is not something that only happens when the powers-that-be accept our solution – when we give that ball a push or clear the barriers out of the way (in the high school physics problem of Chapter 5). It can happen in every interaction we have with any other human being.

We give a compliment. We show respect. We mention a recent job opening. We talk to someone we might normally avoid. We put someone in touch with the help they need. We let people stay in our house until they get back on their feet. These actions and many others offer a path to the better world we all desire, and we can walk that path every day.

I wrote this book not to answer the question, *How do we eradicate poverty?* but rather, *What am I, as a human being, to do, living as I do in a world where poverty exists?* This is my answer: To accept the world as it is and to uphold the dignity of the human experience and of all those with whom I share it. To give readily of what I have in time, talent, and treasure. To look in every interaction for how I might put my gifts in the service of others. To look deeply at my emotions to hear their messages for my own life and for my work in the world, and to know the difference between the two. To act from joy, to experience awe, and to nurture a deep faith that one day we shall attain the object of our longing.

BIBLIOGRAPHY

Acemoglu, Daron, and James A. Robinson. *Why Nations Fail: The Origins of Power, Prosperity, and Poverty*. New York: Crown Business, 2012.

Alcindor, Yamiche. "Ben Carson Calls Poverty a 'State of Mind,' Igniting a Backlash." *New York Times*, May 25, 2017. Accessed October 15, 2018. https://www.nytimes.com/2017/05/25/us/politics/ben-carson-poverty-hud-state-of-mind.html.

Arend, Elizabeth D. "Ben Carson and the Poverty 'State of Mind'" (Letter to the editor). *New York Times*, May 26, 2017. Accessed October 15, 2018. https://www.nytimes.com/2017/05/26/opinion/ben-carson-and-the-poverty-state-of-mind.html.

Badger, Emily. "Does 'Wrong Mind-Set' Cause Poverty or Vice Versa?" *New York Times*, May 30, 2017. Accessed October 15, 2018. https://www.nytimes.com/2017/05/30/upshot/ben-carsons-thinking-and-how-poverty-affects-your-state-of-mind.html.

Banerjee, Abhijit V., and Esther Duflo. *Poor Economics: A Radical Rethinking of the Way to Fight Poverty*. New York: PublicAffairs, 2011.

Banfield, Edward C. *The Unheavenly City Revisited*. Long Grove, IL: Waveland Press, Inc., 1990.

Bertrand, Marianne, and Sendhil Mullainathan. *Are Emily and Greg More Employable than Lakisha and Jamal? A Field Experiment on Labor Market Discrimination* (NBER Working Paper No. 9873). Cambridge, MA: National Bureau of Economic Research, 2003.

Bourguignon, François, and Christian Morrisson. "Inequality among World Citizens: 1820-1992." *American Economic Review* 92, no. 4 (September 2002): 727-744.

Bowles, Samuel, Steven N. Durlauf, and Karla Hoff, eds. *Poverty Traps*. New York: Russell Sage Foundation, 2006.

Bregman, Rutger. *Utopia for Realists: How We Can Build the Ideal World*. New York: Little, Brown, and Company, 2017.

Collier, Lorna. "Growth after trauma." *Monitor on Psychology* 47, no. 10 (November 2016). Accessed August 10, 2018. https://www.apa.org/monitor/2016/11/growth-trauma.aspx.

Cuddy, Amy. *Presence: Bringing Your Boldest Self to Your Biggest Challenges*. New York: Back Bay Books, 2015.

D'Amato, Erik. "Mystery of Disgust." *Psychology Today*, January 1998. Accessed October 15, 2018. https://www.psychologytoday.com/us/articles/199801/mystery-disgust.

Diamond, Jared. *Guns, Germs, and Steel: The Fates of Human Societies*. New York: W.W. Norton & Company, 1999.

Diamond, Jared. "What Makes Countries Rich or Poor?" *New York Review of Books*, June 7, 2012. Accessed March 6, 2018. http://www.nybooks.com/articles/2012/06/07/what-makes-countries-rich-or-poor.

DiSalvo, Daniel. "Edward Banfield Revisited." *National Affairs*, Summer 2017.

"Dr. Ben Carson: Poverty Is 'a State of Mind.'" SiriusXM, May 30, 2017. Accessed October 15, 2018. http://blog.siriusxm.com/dr-ben-carson-poverty-is-a-state-of-mind.

Dweck, Carol S. *Mindset: The New Psychology of Success*. New York: Ballantine Books, 2007.

Ekman, Paul. "Basic Emotions." In *Handbook of Cognition and Emotion*, edited by T. Dalgleish and M. Power, 45-60. New York: John Wiley & Sons, Ltd., 1999.

Ekman, Paul. *Emotions Revealed*. New York: St. Martin's Griffin, 2007.

Ellwood, David T. *Poor Support: Poverty in the American Family*. New York: Basic Books, 1988.

Erikson, Erik H. *Insight and Responsibility: Lectures on the Ethical Implications of Psychoanalytic Insight*. New York: W.W. Norton & Company, 1964.

Fessler, Pam. "Housing Secretary Ben Carson Says Poverty Is A 'State Of Mind.'" NPR, May 25, 2017. Accessed October 15, 2018. https://www.npr.org/2017/05/25/530068988/ben-carson-says-poverty-is-a-state-of-mind.

Freire, Paulo. *Pedagogy of the Oppressed*. New York: Penguin Books, 1996.

Galbraith, John Kenneth. *The Nature of Mass Poverty*. Cambridge, MA: Harvard University Press, 1979.

Greenbaum, Susan D. *Blaming the Poor: The Long Shadow of the Moynihan Report on Cruel Images About Poverty*. New Brunswick, NJ: Rutgers University Press, 2015.

Hamedy, Saba. "HUD secretary Ben Carson: Poverty is largely 'a state of mind.'" CNN, May 25, 2017. Accessed August 10, 2018. https://www.cnn.com/2017/05/24/politics/ben-carson-poverty-state-of-mind/index.html.

Harrington, Michael. *The Other America: Poverty in the United States*. New York: Scribner, 2012.

Haskins, Ron, and Isabel Sawhill. *Creating an Opportunity Society*. Washington, DC: The Brookings Institution, 2009.

Herrnstein, Richard J., and Charles Murray. *The Bell Curve: Intelligence and Class Structure in American Life*. New York: Simon and Schuster, 1994.

Heschel, Abraham Joshua. *God in Search of Man: A Philosophy of Judaism*. New York: Farrar, Straus and Giroux, 1976.

Hill, Napoleon. *Think and Grow Rich*. New York: Fawcett Books, 1987.

Holmes, Jamie. "Why Can't More Poor People Escape Poverty?" *New Republic*, June 5, 2011.

Hy, Lê Xuân, and Jane Loevinger. *Measuring Ego Development*. 2nd ed. Mahwah, New Jersey: Lawrence Erlbaum Associates, Publishers, 1996.

Isenberg, Nancy. *White Trash: The 400-Year Untold History of Class in America*. New York: Viking, 2016.

Izard, Carroll E. "The Many Meanings/Aspects of Emotion: Definitions, Functions, Activation, and Regulation." *Emotion Review* 2, no. 4 (October 2010): 363–370.

Jayachandran, Seema. "Think Positive, Climb Out of Poverty? It Just Might Work" *New York Times*, July 13, 2018. Accessed October 17, 2018. https://www.nytimes.com/2018/07/13/business/think-positive-climb-out-of-poverty-it-just-might-work.html.

Johnson, Barry. *Polarity Management: Identifying and Managing Unsolvable Problems*. Amherst, MA: HRD Press, 2014.

Joseph, Jay. *Gene Illusion: Genetic Research in Psychiatry and Psychology Under the Microscope*. New York: Algora Publishing, 2004.

Karelis, Charles. *The Persistence of Poverty: Why the Economics of the Well-Off Can't Help the Poor*. New Haven: Yale University Press, 2007.

Kegan, Robert, and Lisa Laskow Lahey. *Immunity to Change: How to Overcome It and Unlock the Potential in Yourself and Your Organization*. Boston: Harvard Business Press, 2009.

King, Jr., Martin Luther. *Stride Toward Freedom: The Montgomery Story*. New York: Harper & Brothers, Publishers, 1958.

Laplace, Pierre Simon. *A Philosophical Essay on Probabilities*. 6th ed. Translated by Frederick Wilson Truscott and Frederick Lincoln Emory. New York: Dover Publications, Inc., 1951.

Lareau, Annette. *Unequal Childhoods: Class, Race, and Family Life*. 2nd ed. Los Angeles: University of California Press, 2011.

Lasker, Harry. "Ego Development and Motivation: A Cross-Cultural Cognitive-Developmental Analysis of n-Achievement." PhD diss., University of Chicago, 1978.

Leacock, Eleanor Burke, ed. *The Culture of Poverty: A Critique*. New York: Simon and Schuster, 1971.

Lewis, Oscar. *Five Families: Mexican Case Studies in the Culture of Poverty*. New York: Basic Books, 2000.

Lewis, Oscar. "The Culture of Poverty." *Scientific American* 215 no. 4, October 1966.

Lighthill, Sir James. "The Recently Recognized Failure of Predictability in Newtonian Dynamics." *Proceedings of The Royal Society* A 407 (September 1986): 35-50.

Loevinger, Jane, ed. *Technical Foundations for Measuring Ego Development: The Washington University Sentence Completion Test*. Mahwah, NJ: Lawrence Erlbaum Associates, Publishers, 1998.

Loevinger, Jane. *Ego Development: Conceptions and Theories*. Washington, DC:

Jossey-Bass Publishers, 1976.

Lurie, Irene. "Major Changes in the Structure of the AFDC Program Since 1935." *Cornell Law Review* 59 no. 5 (June 1974). Accessed October 15, 2018. https://scholarship.law.cornell.edu/cgi/viewcontent.cgi?article=3953&context=clr.

Madrigal, Alexis C. "The Racist Housing Policy That Made Your Neighborhood." *Atlantic*, May 22, 2014.

McGonigal, Kelly. *The Upside of Stress: Why Stress Is Good for You, and How to Get Good at It*. New York: Penguin Random House LLC, 2015.

McGuire, Joseph T., and Joseph W. Kable. "Decision makers calibrate behavioral persistence on the basis of time-interval experience." *Cognition* 124 (2012): 216–226.

McLaren, Karla. *The Language of Emotions: What Your Feelings Are Trying to Tell You*. Boulder, CO: Sounds True, 2010.

Mead, Lawrence M. *The New Politics of Poverty: The Nonworking Poor in America*. New York: Basic Books, 1992.

Meade, Eric. "What If We Loved the Poor?" *World Future Review*, Spring 2010.

Mishal, Lawrence, and Alyssa Davis. *CEO Pay Continues to Rise as Typical Workers Are Paid Less* (Issue Brief #380). Washington, DC: Economic Policy Institute, June 12, 2014. Accessed October 10, 2018. https://www.epi.org/files/2014/ceo-pay-continues-to-rise.pdf.

Mitchell, Melanie. *Complexity: A Guided Tour*. New York: Oxford University Press, 2009.

Moynihan, Daniel Patrick. *The Negro Family: The Case for National Action*. Washington, DC: Office of Policy Planning and Research, U.S. Department of Labor, 1965.

Moyo, Dambisa. *Dead Aid: Why Aid Is Not Working and How There Is A Better Way For Africa*. New York: Farrar, Straus, and Giroux, 2009.

Mullainathan, Sendhil, and Eldar Shafir. *Scarcity: The New Science of Having Less and How It Defines Our Lives*. New York: Picador, 2013.

Murray, Charles. *Losing Ground: American Social Policy 1950-1980*. 2nd ed. New York: Basic Books, 1994.

Murray, Charles. *In Our Hands: A Plan to Replace the Welfare State*. Washington, DC: The AEI Press, 2006.

Naraya, Deepa, Raj Patel, Kai Schafft, Anne Rademacher, and Sarah Koch-Schulte. *Voices of the Poor: Can Anyone Hear Us?* Washington, DC: The World Bank, 2000.

Noonan, David. "Is Guaranteed Income for All the Answer to Joblessness and Poverty?" *Scientific American*, July 18, 2017. Accessed October 2, 2018. https://www.scientificamerican.com/article/is-guaranteed-income-for-all-the-answer-to-joblessness-and-poverty.

Nova, Annie. "More Americans now support a universal basic income." CNBC, February 26, 2018. Accessed October 4, 2018. https://www.cnbc.com/2018/02/26/roughly-half-of-americans-now-support-universal-basic-income.html.

O'Fallon, Terri, "How Development Shapes Leadership, Systems, and Norms," June 2016, 14. Unpublished paper provided to the author, October 18, 2018.

Payne, Ruby K. *A Framework for Understanding Poverty: A Cognitive Approach.* Rev. ed. Highlands, TX: aha! Process, Inc., 2013.

Polak, Paul. *Out of Poverty: What Works When Traditional Approaches Fail.* New York: Berrett-Koehler Publishers, 2009.

Rainwater, Lee, and William L. Yancey. *The Moynihan Report and the Politics of Controversy.* Cambridge, MA: M.I.T. Press, 1967.

Ramalingam, Ben. *Aid on the Edge of Chaos: Rethinking International Cooperation in a Complex World.* New York: Oxford University Press, 2013.

Rank, Mark R. "Rethinking American Poverty." *Contexts* 10, no. 2 (2011): 16-21.

Raz, Mical. *What's Wrong with the Poor? Psychiatry, Race, and the War on Poverty.* Chapel Hill, NC: The University of North Carolina Press, 2013.

Redeaux, Monique. "The Culture of Poverty Reloaded." *Monthly Review: An Independent Socialist Magazine*, July-August, 2011: 96-102. Accessed July 18, 2018. https://monthlyreview.org/2011/07/01/the-culture-of-poverty-reloaded.

Reed, Touré F. "All Roads Named Culture of Poverty Lead to Mass Incarceration." *Labor: Studies in Working-Class History of the Americas* 14, no. 4 (2017): 75-79. Accessed September 11, 2018. https://muse.jhu.edu.

Reeves, Richard, Edward Rodrigue, and Elizabeth Kneebone. *Five Evils: Multidimensional Poverty and Race in America.* Washington, DC: The Brookings Institution, April 2016.

Riley, James C. "Estimates of Regional and Global Life Expectancy, 1800–2001." *Population and Development Review* 31, no. 3 (September 2005): 537–543.

Robbins, Tony. *Unshakeable.* New York: Simon & Schuster, 2017.

Ropers, Richard H. *Persistent Poverty: The American Dream Turned Nightmare.* New York: Plenum Press, 1991.

Rosenberg, Marshall B. *Nonviolent Communication: A Language of Life.* Encinitas, CA: PuddleDancer Press, 2003.

Roser, Max. "Child Mortality." OurWorldInData.org. Accessed March 14, 2018. https://ourworldindata.org/child-mortality.

Rothman, Joshua. "The Lives of Poor White People." *New Yorker,* September 12, 2016. Accessed October 17, 2018. https://www.newyorker.com/culture/cultural-comment/the-lives-of-poor-white-people.

Ryan, William. *Blaming the Victim.* Rev. ed. New York: Vintage Books, 1976.

Sachs, Jeffrey. *The End of Poverty: Economic Possibilities for Our Time.* New York: Penguin Press, 2005.

Sartre, Jean-Paul. *The Emotions.* Translated by Bernard Frechtman. New York: Philosophical Library, 1948.

Sawhill, Isabel V. "The Behavioral Aspects of Poverty." The Brookings Institution, September 1, 2003. Accessed October 17, 2018. https://www.brookings.edu/articles/the-behavioral-aspects-of-poverty.

Sawhill, Isabel V. *Generation Unbound: Drifting into Sex and Parenthood Without Marriage.* Washington, DC: The Brookings Institution, 2014.

Sen, Amartya. *Development as Freedom.* New York: Anchor Books, 2000.

Sial, Farwa, and Carolina Alves. "Why Positive Thinking Won't Get You Out of Poverty." *Transformation,* September 11, 2018. Accessed October 15, 2018. https://www.opendemocracy.net/transformation/farwa-sial-and-carolina-alves/why-positive-thinking-won-t-get-you-out-of-poverty.

Sincero, Jen. *You Are a Badass: How to Stop Doubting Your Greatness and Start Living an Awesome Life.* Philadelphia: Running Press, 2013.

Strauss, William, and Neil Howe. *Generations: The History of America's Future, 1584-2069.* New York: Morrow, 1991.

Tanner, Jonathan. "Ending World Poverty Is an Unrealistic Goal." *Guardian,* March 11, 2014. Accessed June 8, 2018. https://www.theguardian.com/global-development-professionals-network/2014/mar/11/end-world-poverty-unrealistic-inequality.

Thompson, Derek. "Your Brain on Poverty: Why Poor People Seem to Make Bad Decisions." *Atlantic,* November 22, 2013. Accessed October 15, 2018. https://www.theatlantic.com/business/archive/2013/11/your-brain-on-poverty-why-poor-people-seem-to-make-bad-decisions/281780.

Tucker Carlson Tonight, FOX News, May 25, 2017.

Twist, Lynne. *The Soul of Money: Reclaiming the Wealth of Our Inner Resources.* New York: W.W. Norton & Company, 2017.

UNESCO. *Education for All Global Monitoring Report*, 2006. Accessed August 3, 2018. http://www.unesco.org/education/GMR2006/full/chapt8_eng. pdf.

U.S. Department of Health and Human Services. "Poverty Guidelines." U.S. Federal Register, January 18, 2018. Accessed October 15, 2018. https:// www.federalregister.gov/documents/2018/01/18/2018-00814/annual-update-of-the-hhs-poverty-guidelines.

Vance, J.D. "Consigned to 'Assistance.'" *National Review*, October 20, 2014. Accessed September 22, 2018. https://www.nationalreview. com/2014/10/consigned-assistance-j-d-vance.

Vance, J.D. *Hillbilly Elegy: A Memoir of a Family and Culture in Crisis.* New York: HarperCollins Publishers, 2016.

Voys, Kathleen D., Roy F. Baumeister, Jean M. Twenge, Brandon J. Schmeichel, and Dianne M. Tice. "Decision Fatigue Exhausts Self-Regulatory Resources." *Psychology Today*, 2006. Accessed November 14, 2017. https:// www.psychologytoday.com/files/attachments/584/decision200602-15vohs.pdf.

Weaver, Warren. "Science and Complexity." *American Scientist* 36, no. 4 (October 1948): 536-544.

Welshman, John. *Underclass: A History of the Excluded Since 1880.* 2nd ed. New York: Bloomsbury, 2013.

Wetzel, Deborah. "Bolsa Família: Brazil's Quiet Revolution." World Bank, November 4, 2013. Accessed May 21, 2018. http://www.worldbank.org/ en/news/opinion/2013/11/04/bolsa-familia-Brazil-quiet-revolution.

Whitman, Alden. "Oscar Lewis, Author and Anthropologist, Dead." *New York Times*, December 18, 1970. Accessed July 12, 2018. https://www.nytimes. com/1970/12/18/archives/oscar-lewis-author-and-anthropologist-dead-u-of-illinois-professor.html.

Wilson, William Julius. *The Truly Disadvantaged: The Inner City, the Underclass, and Public Policy.* Chicago: University of Chicago Press, 1987.

Wolff, Edward N. *Household Wealth Trends in the United States, 1962 to 2016: Has Middle Class Wealth Recovered?* (Working Paper No. 24085). Cambridge, MA: National Bureau of Economic Research, November 2017. Accessed

October 15, 2018. http://www.nber.org/papers/w24085.

Wolff, Jonathan, and Avner de-Shalit. *Disadvantage.* New York: Oxford University Press, 2007.

World Bank. *World Development Report: Mind, Society, Behavior.* Washington, DC: World Bank Group. Accessed November 14, 2017. http://documents.worldbank.org/curated/en/645741468339541646/pdf/928630WDR0978100Box385358B00PUBLIC0.pdf.

World Bank. *Taking On Inequality (Poverty and Shared Prosperity 2016).* Washington, DC: World Bank Group, 2016.

Endnotes

Introduction

1. François Bourguignon and Christian Morrisson, "Inequality among World Citizens: 1820-1992," *American Economic Review* 92, no. 4 (September 2002): 731.

Chapter One

1. "Dr. Ben Carson: Poverty Is 'a State of Mind,'" SiriusXM, May 30, 2017, accessed October 15, 2018, http://blog.siriusxm.com/dr-ben-carson-poverty-is-a-state-of-mind.

2. Pam Fessler, "Housing Secretary Ben Carson Says Poverty Is A 'State Of Mind,'" NPR, May 25, 2017, accessed October 15, 2018, https://www.npr.org/2017/05/25/530068988/ben-carson-says-poverty-is-a-state-of-mind.

3. Elizabeth D. Arend, "Ben Carson and the Poverty 'State of Mind'" (Letter to the editor), *New York Times*, May 26, 2017, accessed October 15, 2018, https://www.nytimes.com/2017/05/26/opinion/ben-carson-and-the-poverty-state-of-mind.html.

4. Pam Fessler, "Housing Secretary Ben Carson Says Poverty Is A 'State Of Mind,'" NPR, May 25, 2017, accessed October 15, 2018, https://www.npr.org/2017/05/25/530068988/ben-carson-says-poverty-is-a-state-of-mind.

5. *Tucker Carlson Tonight*, FOX News, May 25, 2017.
6. Emily Badger, "Does 'Wrong Mind-Set' Cause Poverty or Vice Versa?" *New York Times*, May 30, 2017, accessed October 15, 2018, https://www.nytimes.com/2017/05/30/upshot/ben-carsons-thinking-and-how-poverty-affects-your-state-of-mind.html.
7. Derek Thompson, "Your Brain on Poverty: Why Poor People Seem to Make Bad Decisions," *Atlantic*, Nov. 22, 2013, accessed October 15, 2018, https://www.theatlantic.com/business/archive/2013/11/your-brain-on-poverty-why-poor-people-seem-to-make-bad-decisions/281780.
8. Oscar Lewis, *Five Families: Mexican Case Studies in the Culture of Poverty* (New York: Basic Books, 2000).
9. William Ryan, *Blaming the Victim*, Rev. ed. (New York: Vintage Books, 1976).
10. John Kenneth Galbraith, *The Nature of Mass Poverty* (Cambridge, MA: Harvard University Press, 1979), 1.
11. "Poverty," World Bank, accessed October 15, 2018, https://data.worldbank.org/topic/poverty.
12. Different levels exist for residents of Alaska and Hawaii. "Annual Update of the HHS Poverty Guidelines," Federal Register, January 18, 2018, accessed October 17, 2018, https://www.federalregister.gov/documents/2018/01/18/2018-00814/annual-update-of-the-hhs-poverty-guidelines.
13. "2018 Global Multidimensional Poverty Index," United Nations, accessed October 15, 2018, http://hdr.undp.org/en/2018-MPI.
14. Carroll E. Izard, "The Many Meanings/Aspects of Emotion: Definitions, Functions, Activation, and Regulation," *Emotion Review* 2, no. 4 (October 2010): 367.
15. Deepa Naraya et al., *Voices of the Poor: Can Anyone Hear Us?* (Washington, DC: The World Bank, 2000).
16. Adapted from Pam Fessler, "One Family's Story Shows How The Cycle Of Poverty Is Hard To Break," NPR, May 7, 2014, accessed October 15, 2018, https://www.npr.org/2014/05/07/309734339/one-familys-story-shows-how-the-cycle-of-poverty-is-hard-to-break.
17. Adapted from Jamie Anderson and Wajiha Ahmed, *Smallholder Diaries: Building the Evidence Base with Farming Families in Mozambique, Tanzania, and Pakistan* (Washington, DC: Consultative Group to Assist the Poor, 2016), accessed October 15, 2018, http://www.cgap.org/research/publication/financial-diaries-smallholder-families.
18. Paul Ekman, "Basic Emotions," in *Handbook of Cognition and Emotion*, ed. T. Dalgleish and M. Power (New York: John Wiley & Sons, Ltd., 1999), 45-60.
19. "Atlas of Emotions," accessed October 15, 2018, http://www.atlasofemotions.org.
20. Paul Ekman, *Emotions Revealed* (New York: St. Martin's Griffin, 2007), 39.
21. Ibid., 41.

22. *Inside Out*, directed by Pete Docter and Ronnie Del Carmen (Pixar Animation Studios and Walt Disney Pictures, 2015).

23. John Kenneth Galbraith, *The Nature of Mass Poverty* (Cambridge, MA: Harvard University Press, 1979), 41.

24. World Bank, *World Development Report: Mind, Society, Behavior* (Washington, DC: World Bank Group, 2015), 18-19, accessed November 14, 2017, http://documents.worldbank.org/curated/en/645741468339541646/pdf/928630WDR0 978100Box385358B00PUBLIC0.pdf.

25. Marianne Bertrand and Sendhil Mullainathan, *Are Emily and Greg More Employable than Lakisha and Jamal? A Field Experiment on Labor Market Discrimination* (NBER Working Paper No. 9873) (Cambridge, MA: National Bureau of Economic Research, 2003), accessed October 15, 2018, http://www.nber.org/papers/w9873.

Chapter Two

1. Two weeks later, Carson moderated his comments in an interview with NPR, saying that one's state of mind is just one factor in poverty, but an important factor. Notably, he disagreed with the article cited herein (Badger 2017) that provides the Gary Evans quote regarding the effects of poverty on brain development. See Pam Fessler, "Housing Secretary Ben Carson Clarifies Comment That Poverty Is A 'State Of Mind,'" NPR, June 5, 2017, accessed October 15, 2018, https://www.npr.org/2017/06/05/531461142/housing-secretary-ben-carson-clarifies-comment-that-poverty-is-a-state-of-mind.

2. Daniel Patrick Moynihan, *The Negro Family: The Case for National Action* (Washington, DC: Office of Policy Planning and Research, U.S. Department of Labor, 1965).

3. Saba Hamedy, "HUD secretary Ben Carson: Poverty is largely 'a state of mind,'" CNN, May 25, 2017, accessed October 15, 2018, https://www.cnn.com/2017/05/24/politics/ben-carson-poverty-state-of-mind/index.html.Hamedy 2017.

4. Ron Haskins and Isabel Sawhill, *Creating an Opportunity Society* (Washington, DC: The Brookings Institution, 2009), 4.

5. Ibid., 70.

6. Ibid., 4.

7. J.D. Vance, *Hillbilly Elegy: A Memoir of a Family and Culture in Crisis* (New York: HarperCollins Publishers, 2016), 6-7, emphasis original.

8. John Welshman, *Underclass: A History of the Excluded Since 1880*, 2nd ed. (New York: Bloomsbury, 2013), 30.

9. *Buck v. Bell*, 274 U.S. 200 (1927).

10. Richard J. Herrnstein and Charles Murray, *The Bell Curve: Intelligence and Class Structure in American Life* (New York: Simon and Schuster, 1994), 311.

11. John Welshman, *Underclass: A History of the Excluded Since 1880*, 2nd ed.

(New York: Bloomsbury, 2013), 74-75.

12. Jay Joseph, *Gene Illusion: Genetic Research in Psychiatry and Psychology Under the Microscope* (New York: Algora Publishing, 2004).

13. Sendhil Mullainathan and Eldar Shafir, *Scarcity: The New Science of Having Less and How It Defines Our Lives* (New York: Picador, 2013).

14. Melanie Mitchell, *Complexity: A Guided Tour* (New York: Oxford University Press, 2009), 276.

15. Charles Murray, *In Our Hands: A Plan to Replace the Welfare State* (Washington, DC: The AEI Press, 2006), 2-3.

16. Charles Murray, *Losing Ground: American Social Policy, 1950-1980,* 2nd ed. (New York: Basic Books, 1994).

17. Irene Lurie, "Major Changes in the Structure of the AFDC Program Since 1935," *Cornell Law Review* 59, no. 5 (June 1974): 832, accessed October 15, 2018, https://scholarship.law.cornell.edu/cgi/viewcontent. cgi?article=3953&context=clr.

18. Dambisa Moyo, *Dead Aid: Why Aid Is Not Working and How There Is A Better Way For Africa* (New York: Farrar, Straus, and Giroux, 2009).

19. Ibid., 49.

20. John Welshman, *Underclass: A History of the Excluded Since 1880,* 2nd ed. (New York: Bloomsbury, 2013), 19.

21. David T. Ellwood, *Poor Support: Poverty in the American Family* (New York: Basic Books, 1988), 6.

22. Ron Haskins and Isabel Sawhill, *Creating an Opportunity Society* (Washington, DC: The Brookings Institution, 2009), 1-2.

23. Lawrence M. Mead, *The New Politics of Poverty: The Nonworking Poor in America* (New York: Basic Books, 1992), 13.

24. Richard J. Herrnstein and Charles Murray, *The Bell Curve: Intelligence and Class Structure in American Life* (New York: Simon and Schuster, 1994), 523.

25. Isabel V. Sawhill, "The Behavioral Aspects of Poverty," The Brookings Institution, September 1, 2003, accessed October 15, 2018, https://www. brookings.edu/articles/the-behavioral-aspects-of-poverty.

26. Mark Robert Rank and Thomas A. Hirschl, "Poverty Risk Calculator," Confronting Poverty, accessed October 15, 2018, https://confrontingpoverty. org/poverty-risk-calculator.

27. Mark R. Rank, "Rethinking American Poverty," *Contexts* 10, no. 2 (2011): 18.

28. Richard Reeves, Edward Rodrigue, and Elizabeth Kneebone, *Five Evils: Multidimensional Poverty and Race in America* (Washington, DC: The Brookings Institution, April 2016), 7-8.

29. Alexis C. Madrigal, "The Racist Housing Policy That Made Your Neighborhood," *Atlantic*, May 22, 2014, accessed October 15, 2018, https:// www.theatlantic.com/business/archive/2014/05/the-racist-housing-policy-that-made-your-neighborhood/371439.

30. Amartya Sen, *Development as Freedom* (New York: Anchor Books, 2000), 75.
31. "Human Development Index (HDI)," United Nations, accessed October 15, 2018, http://hdr.undp.org/en/content/human-development-index-hdi.
32. "2018 Global Multidimensional Poverty Index," United Nations, accessed October 15, 2018, http://hdr.undp.org/en/2018-MPI.
33. Amartya Sen, *Development as Freedom* (New York: Anchor Books, 2000), 53.
34. Jonathan Wolff and Avner de-Shalit, *Disadvantage* (New York: Oxford University Press, 2007), 80.
35. Ibid., 80.
36. Ibid., 47.
37. Jeffrey Sachs, *The End of Poverty: Economic Possibilities for Our Time* (New York: The Penguin Press, 2005), 19.
38. Samuel Bowles, Steven N. Durlauf, and Karla Hoff, eds., *Poverty Traps* (New York: Russell Sage Foundation, 2006), 2.
39. Jeffrey Sachs, *The End of Poverty: Economic Possibilities for Our Time* (New York: The Penguin Press, 2005), 73.
40. John Kenneth Galbraith, *The Nature of Mass Poverty* (Cambridge, MA: Harvard University Press, 1979).
41. Daron Acemoglu and James A. Robinson, *Why Nations Fail: The Origins of Power, Prosperity, and Poverty* (New York: Crown Business, 2012), 43.
42. Ibid., 75.
43. Ibid., 68.
44. Paul Polak, *Out of Poverty: What Works When Traditional Approaches Fail* (New York: Berrett-Koehler Publishers, 2009).
45. Jonathan Wolff and Avner de-Shalit, *Disadvantage* (New York: Oxford University Press, 2007), 2.
46. Ibid., 8.
47. Ibid., 7.
48. Charles Karelis, *The Persistence of Poverty: Why the Economics of the Well-Off Can't Help the Poor* (New Haven: Yale University Press, 2007).
49. Joseph T. McGuire and Joseph W. Kable, "Decision makers calibrate behavioral persistence on the basis of time-interval experience," *Cognition* 124 (2012): 216–226.
50. Abhijit V. Banerjee and Esther Duflo, *Poor Economics: A Radical Rethinking of the Way to Fight Poverty* (New York: PublicAffairs, 2011), 38.
51. World Bank, *World Development Report: Mind, Society, Behavior* (Washington, DC: World Bank Group, 2015), 80, accessed November 14, 2017, http://documents.worldbank.org/curated/en/645741468339541646/pdf/928630WDR0 978100Box385358B00PUBLIC0.pdf.
52. Sendhil Mullainathan and Eldar Shafir, *Scarcity: The New Science of Having Less and How It Defines Our Lives* (New York: Picador, 2013), 148.
53. Ibid.

54. Kathleen D. Voys et al., "Decision Fatigue Exhausts Self-Regulatory Resources," *Psychology Today*, 2006, accessed November 14, 2017, https://www.psychologytoday.com/files/attachments/584/decision200602-15vohs.pdf.

55. Rutger Bregman, *Utopia for Realists: How We Can Build the Ideal World* (New York: Little, Brown, and Company, 2017).

56. Mical Raz, *What's Wrong with the Poor?: Psychiatry, Race, and the War on Poverty* (Chapel Hill, NC: The University of North Carolina Press, 2013), 30.

57. David Noonan, "Is Guaranteed Income for All the Answer to Joblessness and Poverty?," *Scientific American*, July 18, 2017, accessed October 15, 2018, https://www.scientificamerican.com/article/is-guaranteed-income-for-all-the-answer-to-joblessness-and-poverty.

58. Annie Nova, "More Americans now support a universal basic income," CNBC, February 26, 2018, accessed October 15, 2018, https://www.cnbc.com/2018/02/26/roughly-half-of-americans-now-support-universal-basic-income.html.

59. Jamie Holmes, "Why Can't More Poor People Escape Poverty?," *New Republic*, June 5, 2011.

60. Deborah Wetzel, "Bolsa Família: Brazil's Quiet Revolution," World Bank, November 4, 2013, accessed May 21, 2018, http://www.worldbank.org/en/news/opinion/2013/11/04/bolsa-familia-Brazil-quiet-revolution.

61. Abhijit V. Banerjee and Esther Duflo, *Poor Economics: A Radical Rethinking of the Way to Fight Poverty* (New York: PublicAffairs, 2011), 25.

62. Sendhil Mullainathan and Eldar Shafir, *Scarcity: The New Science of Having Less and How It Defines Our Lives* (New York: Picador, 2013), 150-155.

63. Ibid., 161.

64. Abhijit V. Banerjee and Esther Duflo, *Poor Economics: A Radical Rethinking of the Way to Fight Poverty* (New York: PublicAffairs, 2011), x.

65. Ibid., 33.

66. John Welshman, *Underclass: A History of the Excluded Since 1880*, 2nd ed. (New York: Bloomsbury, 2013), 19.

67. Ibid., 20.

68. Oscar Lewis, "The Culture of Poverty," *Scientific American* 215, no. 4 (October 1966): 19.

69. Ibid., 19.

70. Ibid.

71. Michael Harrington, *The Other America: Poverty in the United States* (New York: Scribner, 2012), 135.

72. Oscar Lewis, "The Culture of Poverty," *Scientific American* 215, no. 4 (October 1966): 19.

73. William Julius Wilson, *The Truly Disadvantaged: The Inner City, the Underclass, and Public Policy* (Chicago: University of Chicago Press, 1987), 3-13.

74. Edward C. Banfield, *The Unheavenly City Revisited* (Long Grove, IL: Waveland Press, Inc., 1990), 53.
75. Ibid., 62.
76. John Kenneth Galbraith, *The Nature of Mass Poverty* (Cambridge, MA: Harvard University Press, 1979).
77. Michael Harrington, *The Other America: Poverty in the United States* (New York: Scribner, 2012), 137.
78. John Kenneth Galbraith, *The Nature of Mass Poverty* (Cambridge, MA: Harvard University Press, 1979), 94.
79. Ruby K. Payne, *A Framework for Understanding Poverty: A Cognitive Approach*, Rev. ed. (Highlands, TX: aha! Process, Inc., 2013), 10.
80. Ibid., 67.
81. Ibid., 54-55.
82. Annette Lareau, *Unequal Childhoods: Class, Race, and Family Life*, 2nd ed. (Los Angeles: University of California Press, 2011), 1-2.
83. Ibid., 3.
84. Ibid., 3.
85. Ibid., 3.
86. Oscar Lewis, "The Culture of Poverty," *Scientific American* 215, no. 4 (October 1966): 23.
87. Alden Whitman, "Oscar Lewis, Author and Anthropologist, Dead," *New York Times*, December 18, 1970, accessed October 15, 2018, https://www.nytimes.com/1970/12/18/archives/oscar-lewis-author-and-anthropologist-dead-u-of-illinois-professor.html.
88. Oscar Lewis, "The Culture of Poverty," *Scientific American* 215, no. 4 (October 1966): 19.

Chapter Three

1. Touré F. Reed, "All Roads Named Culture of Poverty Lead to Mass Incarceration," *Labor: Studies in Working-Class History of the Americas* 14, no. 4 (2017): 75-79.
2. J.D. Vance, "Consigned to 'Assistance,'" *National Review*, October 20, 2014, accessed October 15, 2018, https://www.nationalreview.com/2014/10/consigned-assistance-j-d-vance.
3. Alden Whitman, "Oscar Lewis, Author and Anthropologist, Dead," *New York Times*, December 18, 1970, accessed October 15, 2018, https://www.nytimes.com/1970/12/18/archives/oscar-lewis-author-and-anthropologist-dead-u-of-illinois-professor.html.
4. Sendhil Mullainathan and Eldar Shafir, *Scarcity: The New Science of Having Less and How It Defines Our Lives* (New York: Picador, 2013), 153-154.
5. Abhijit V. Banerjee and Esther Duflo, *Poor Economics: A Radical Rethinking of the Way to Fight Poverty* (New York: PublicAffairs, 2011), 229.

6. Susan D. Greenbaum, *Blaming the Poor: The Long Shadow of the Moynihan Report on Cruel Images About Poverty* (New Brunswick, NJ: Rutgers University Press, 2015), 130.
7. William Ryan, *Blaming the Victim*, Rev. ed. (New York: Vintage Books, 1976), 251.
8. Paulo Freire, *Pedagogy of the Oppressed* (New York: Penguin Books, 1996), 43-44.
9. Eleanor Burke Leacock, ed., *The Culture of Poverty: A Critique* (New York: Simon and Schuster, 1971), 7.
10. Monique Redeaux, "The Culture of Poverty Reloaded," *Monthly Review: An Independent Socialist Magazine*, July-August 2011, 100, accessed October 15, 2018, https://monthlyreview.org/2011/07/01/the-culture-of-poverty-reloaded.
11. William Ryan, *Blaming the Victim*, Rev. ed. (New York: Vintage Books, 1976), 23.
12. "Don't trust anyone over 30, unless it's Jack Weinberg," *Berkeley (CA) Daily Planet*, April 6, 2000, accessed October 15, 2018, http://www.berkeleydailyplanet.com/issue/2000-04-06/article/759.
13. William Strauss and Neil Howe, *Generations: The History of America's Future, 1584-2069* (New York: Morrow, 1991).
14. Martin Luther King, Jr., *Stride Toward Freedom: The Montgomery Story* (New York: Harper & Brothers, Publishers, 1958), 212.
15. Susan D. Greenbaum, *Blaming the Poor: The Long Shadow of the Moynihan Report on Cruel Images About Poverty* (New Brunswick, NJ: Rutgers University Press, 2015), 44.
16. William Ryan, *Blaming the Victim*, Rev. ed. (New York: Vintage Books, 1976), 140.
17. Lawrence M. Mead, *The New Politics of Poverty: The Nonworking Poor in America* (New York: Basic Books, 1992).
18. Lawrence Mishal and Alyssa Davis, *CEO Pay Continues to Rise as Typical Workers Are Paid Less* (Issue Brief #380) (Washington, DC: Economic Policy Institute, June 12, 2014), accessed October 15, 2018, https://www.epi.org/files/2014/ceo-pay-continues-to-rise.pdf.
19. Edward N. Wolff, *Household Wealth Trends in the United States, 1962 to 2016: Has Middle Class Wealth Recovered?* (Working Paper No. 24085) (Cambridge, MA: National Bureau of Economic Research, November 2017), accessed October 15, 2018, http://www.nber.org/papers/w24085.
20. Ron Haskins and Isabel Sawhill, *Creating an Opportunity Society* (Washington, DC: The Brookings Institution, 2009), 1-2.
21. David T. Ellwood, *Poor Support: Poverty in the American Family* (New York: Basic Books, 1988), 11, emphasis added.
22. Tony Robbins, *Unshakeable* (New York: Simon & Schuster, 2017), 170-171.
23. Lynne Twist, *The Soul of Money: Reclaiming the Wealth of Our Inner*

Resources (New York: W.W. Norton & Company, 2003), 74-76.

24. Jen Sincero, *You Are a Badass: How to Stop Doubting Your Greatness and Start Living an Awesome Life* (Philadelphia: Running Press, 2013), 208.

25. Napoleon Hill, *Think and Grow Rich* (New York: Fawcett Books, 1987).

26. Carol S. Dweck, *Mindset: The New Psychology of Success* (New York: Ballantine Books, 2007).

27. Kelly McGonigal, *The Upside of Stress: Why Stress Is Good for You, and How to Get Good at It* (New York: Penguin Random House LLC, 2015).

28. Lorna Collier, "Growth After Trauma," *Monitor on Psychology* 47, no. 10 (November 2016), accessed October 15, 2018, https://www.apa.org/monitor/2016/11/growth-trauma.aspx.

29. Ibid.

30. Amy Cuddy, *Presence: Bringing Your Boldest Self to Your Biggest Challenges* (New York: Back Bay Books, 2015).

31. William Ryan, *Blaming the Victim*, Rev. ed. (New York: Vintage Books, 1976), 246.

32. David T. Ellwood, *Poor Support: Poverty in the American Family* (New York: Basic Books, 1988), 215-216.

33. William Ryan, *Blaming the Victim*, Rev. ed. (New York: Vintage Books, 1976), 246.

34. Farwa Sial and Carolina Alves, "Why Positive Thinking Won't Get You Out of Poverty," *Transformation*, September 11, 2018, accessed October 15, 2018, https://www.opendemocracy.net/transformation/farwa-sial-and-carolina-alves/why-positive-thinking-won-t-get-you-out-of-poverty.

35. David T. Ellwood, *Poor Support: Poverty in the American Family* (New York: Basic Books, 1988), 213.

36. Lee Rainwater and William L. Yancey, *The Moynihan Report and the Politics of Controversy* (Cambridge, MA: The M.I.T. Press, 1967), 4.

37. Ibid., 136.

38. Ibid., 130.

39. Ibid., 139.

40. Susan D. Greenbaum, *Blaming the Poor: The Long Shadow of the Moynihan Report on Cruel Images About Poverty* (New Brunswick, NJ: Rutgers University Press, 2015), 2-3.

41. Daniel Patrick Moynihan, *The Negro Family: The Case for National Action* (Washington, DC: Office of Policy Planning and Research, U.S. Department of Labor, 1965).

42. Susan D. Greenbaum, *Blaming the Poor: The Long Shadow of the Moynihan Report on Cruel Images About Poverty* (New Brunswick, NJ: Rutgers University Press, 2015), 1.

Chapter Four

1. Barry Johnson, *Polarity Management: Identifying and Managing Unsolvable Problems* (Amherst, MA: HRD Press, 2014).
2. Clyde Kluckhohn and Henry A. Murray, 1953, *Personality in Nature, Society, and Culture*, 2nd ed. (Reprint, New York: Knopf, 1961), 53.
3. "That's because sympathy that fails to recognize culpability also fails to recognize potentiality." Joshua Rothman, "The Lives of Poor White People," *New Yorker*, September 12, 2016, accessed October 17, 2018, https://www. newyorker.com/culture/cultural-comment/the-lives-of-poor-white-people.
4. Jean-Paul Sartre, *The Emotions*, trans. Bernard Frechtman (New York: Philosophical Library, 1948).
5. J.D. Vance, *Hillbilly Elegy: A Memoir of a Family and Culture in Crisis* (New York: HarperCollins Publishers, 2016), 253.
6. "Alcoholics Anonymous (AA)," Alcohol.org, accessed October 15, 2018, https://www.alcohol.org/alcoholics-anonymous.
7. Erik D'Amato. "Mystery of Disgust," *Psychology Today*, January 1998, accessed October 15, 2018, https://www.psychologytoday.com/us/ articles/199801/mystery-disgust.
8. Abhijit V. Banerjee and Esther Duflo, *Poor Economics: A Radical Rethinking of the Way to Fight Poverty* (New York: PublicAffairs, 2011), x.
9. Ibid., 25.
10. Paul Ekman, *Emotions Revealed* (New York: St. Martin's Griffin, 2007), 124.
11. Mahatma Gandhi, *The Words of Gandhi* (New York: Newmarket Press, 2000), 3.
12. Paulo Freire, *Pedagogy of the Oppressed* (New York: Penguin Books, 1996).

Chapter Five

1. Pierre Simon Laplace, *A Philosophical Essay on Probabilities*, 6th ed., trans. Frederick Wilson Truscott and Frederick Lincoln Emory (New York: Dover Publications, Inc., 1951), 4.
2. Warren Weaver, "Science and Complexity," *American Scientist* 36, no. 4 (October 1948): 536.
3. Sir James Lighthill, "The Recently Recognized Failure of Predictability in Newtonian Dynamics," *Proceedings of The Royal Society* A 407 (September 1986): 38.
4. Ron Haskins and Isabel Sawhill, *Creating an Opportunity Society* (Washington, DC: The Brookings Institution, 2009), 4.
5. Lawrence M. Mead, *The New Politics of Poverty: The Nonworking Poor in America* (New York: Basic Books, 1992), 56.
6. Amartya Sen, *Development as Freedom* (New York: Anchor Books, 2000), 53.
7. Jonathan Wolff and Avner de-Shalit, *Disadvantage* (New York: Oxford University Press, 2007), 80.

8. Purchasing Power Parity (PPP) provides for economic comparisons across countries by correcting for variation in the price of goods and services.
9. Abhijit V. Banerjee and Esther Duflo, *Poor Economics: A Radical Rethinking of the Way to Fight Poverty* (New York: PublicAffairs, 2011), ix.
10. Ibid., 36.
11. Ibid., 33.
12. Ibid., 229.
13. Lawrence M. Mead, *The New Politics of Poverty: The Nonworking Poor in America* (New York: Basic Books, 1992), 136.
14. Oscar Lewis, "The Culture of Poverty," *Scientific American* 215, no. 4 (October 1966): 21.
15. Dambisa Moyo, *Dead Aid: Why Aid Is Not Working and How There Is A Better Way For Africa* (New York: Farrar, Straus, and Giroux, 2009), 52.

Chapter Six
1. Yamiche Alcindor, "Ben Carson Calls Poverty a 'State of Mind,' Igniting a Backlash," *New York Times*, May 25, 2017, accessed October 15, 2018, https://www.nytimes.com/2017/05/25/us/politics/ben-carson-poverty-hud-state-of-mind.html.
2. David T. Ellwood, *Poor Support: Poverty in the American Family* (New York: Basic Books, 1988), 212.
3. Mical Raz, *What's Wrong with the Poor?: Psychiatry, Race, and the War on Poverty* (Chapel Hill, NC: The University of North Carolina Press, 2013).
4. Emily Badger, "Does 'Wrong Mind-Set' Cause Poverty or Vice Versa?" *New York Times*, May 30, 2017, accessed October 15, 2018, https://www.nytimes.com/2017/05/30/upshot/ben-carsons-thinking-and-how-poverty-affects-your-state-of-mind.html.
5. Seema Jayachandran, "Think Positive, Climb Out of Poverty? It Just Might Work," *New York Times*, July 13, 2018, accessed October 15, 2018, https://www.nytimes.com/2018/07/13/business/think-positive-climb-out-of-poverty-it-just-might-work.html.
6. For a complete discussion of this example, see Melanie Mitchell, *Complexity: A Guided Tour* (New York: Oxford University Press, 2009), 27-34.
7. Emily Badger, "Does 'Wrong Mind-Set' Cause Poverty or Vice Versa?" *New York Times*, May 30, 2017, accessed October 15, 2018, https://www.nytimes.com/2017/05/30/upshot/ben-carsons-thinking-and-how-poverty-affects-your-state-of-mind.html.
8. Abhijit V. Banerjee and Esther Duflo, *Poor Economics: A Radical Rethinking of the Way to Fight Poverty* (New York: PublicAffairs, 2011), 31.
9. Richard Meade, e-mail message to the author, May 5, 2018.
10. Jared Diamond, *Guns, Germs, and Steel: The Fates of Human Societies* (New York: W.W. Norton & Company, 1999).

11. I remember playing the video game "Sid Meier's Civilization II" in college, in which you start as a settler in the year 4000 B.C. with the goal of developing a global civilization. If my settler did not find an especially productive resource, like buffalo, whales, or wheat, within the first few turns, I would end that game and start over, since I knew that the other civilizations would get out ahead and I would have no chance to catch up.

12. William Blake, "Auguries of Innocence," in *The Poetical Works of William Blake,* ed. John Sampson (Reprint, New York: Oxford University Press, 1961), 171.

Chapter Seven

1. The Washington University Sentence Completion Test is a projective assessment, which means that it provides an opportunity for respondents to project their own way of thinking so that it can be assessed by the rater. The test consists of 36 sentence roots, such as, "What gets me into trouble is ..." and "A man feels good when ...", which the respondent completes any way they choose. Their sentences are then compared to a scoring manual that lists past responses categorized by ego stage. Lê Xuân Hy and Jane Loevinger, *Measuring Ego Development,* 2nd ed. (Mahwah, New Jersey: Lawrence Erlbaum Associates, Publishers, 1996).

2. Lê Xuân Hy and Jane Loevinger, *Measuring Ego Development,* 2nd ed. (Mahwah, New Jersey: Lawrence Erlbaum Associates, Publishers, 1996), 4-7.

3. Jane Loevinger et al., "Ego Development as a Stage-Type Theory and a Process," in *Technical Foundations for Measuring Ego Development: The Washington University Sentence Completion Test,* ed. Jane Loevinger (Mahwah, NJ: Lawrence Erlbaum Associates, Publishers, 1998), 50.

4. Robert Kegan and Lisa Laskow Lahey, *Immunity to Change: How to Overcome It and Unlock the Potential in Yourself and Your Organization* (Boston: Harvard Business Press, 2009), 51-53.

5. Jane Loevinger, *Ego Development: Conceptions and Theories* (Washington, DC: Jossey-Bass Publishers, 1976), 415.

6. Jane Loevinger et al., "Ego Development as a Stage-Type Theory and a Process," in *Technical Foundations for Measuring Ego Development: The Washington University Sentence Completion Test,* ed. Jane Loevinger (Mahwah, NJ: Lawrence Erlbaum Associates, Publishers, 1998), 50-51.

7. Janet Castro, "Untapped verbal fluency in Black schoolchildren," in *The Culture of Poverty: A Critique,* ed. Eleanor Burke Leacock (New York: Simon and Schuster, 1971), 82.

8. Ruby K. Payne, *A Framework for Understanding Poverty: A Cognitive Approach,* Rev. ed. (Highlands, TX: aha! Process, Inc., 2013), 58.

9. Oscar Lewis, "The Culture of Poverty," *Scientific American* 215, no. 4 (October 1966): 21.

10. P. Michiel Westenberg, Philip D.A. Treffers, and Martine J. Drewes, "A New Version of the WUSCT: The Sentence Completion Test for Children and Youths (SCT-Y)," in *Technical Foundations for Measuring Ego Development: The Washington Sentence Completion Test*, ed. Jane Loevinger (Mahwah, NJ: Lawrence Erlbaum Associates, Publishers, 1998), 88.

11. Harry Lasker, "Ego Development and Motivation: A Cross-Cultural Cognitive Developmental Analysis of n-Achievement," (PhD diss., University of Chicago, 1978), 125.

12. Harry Lasker, "Ego Development and Motivation: A Cross-Cultural Cognitive-Developmental Analysis of n-Achievement," (PhD diss., University of Chicago, 1978), 281.

13. "Dr. Ben Carson: Poverty Is 'a State of Mind,'" SiriusXM, May 30, 2017, accessed October 15, 2018, http://blog.siriusxm.com/dr-ben-carson-poverty-is-a-state-of-mind.

14. Lawrence M. Mead, *The New Politics of Poverty: The Nonworking Poor in America* (New York: Basic Books, 1992), 136.

15. Jane Loevinger et al., "Ego Development as a Stage-Type Theory and a Process," in *Technical Foundations for Measuring Ego Development: The Washington University Sentence Completion Test*, ed. Jane Loevinger (Mahwah, NJ: Lawrence Erlbaum Associates, Publishers, 1998), 52.

16. Lê Xuân Hy and Jane Loevinger, *Measuring Ego Development*. 2nd ed. (Mahwah, New Jersey: Lawrence Erlbaum Associates, Publishers, 1996), 6.

17. Jane Loevinger, *Ego Development: Conceptions and Theories* (Washington, DC: Jossey-Bass Publishers, 1976), 20-21.

18. Ron Haskins and Isabel Sawhill, *Creating an Opportunity Society* (Washington, DC: The Brookings Institution, 2009).

19. J.D. Vance, *Hillbilly Elegy: A Memoir of a Family and Culture in Crisis* (New York: HarperCollins Publishers, 2016), 156-165.

20. Jane Loevinger, *Ego Development: Conceptions and Theories* (Washington, DC: Jossey-Bass Publishers, 1976), 415.

Chapter Eight

1. A bilateral kinship system is one in which both the mother's and father's relatives are equally important in emotional and financial terms.

2. Oscar Lewis, "The Culture of Poverty," *Scientific American* 215, no. 4 (October 1966): 21.

3. Ibid., 23.

4. Michael Harrington, *The Other America: Poverty in the United States* (New York: Scribner, 2012), 96-97.

5. Lawrence M. Mead, *The New Politics of Poverty: The Nonworking Poor in America* (New York: Basic Books, 1992), 147.

6. Edward C. Banfield, *The Unheavenly City Revisited* (Long Grove, IL:

Waveland Press, Inc., 1990), 67.

7. Jane Loevinger et al., "Ego Development as a Stage-Type Theory and a Process," in *Technical Foundations for Measuring Ego Development: The Washington University Sentence Completion Test*, ed. Jane Loevinger (Mahwah, NJ: Lawrence Erlbaum Associates, Publishers, 1998), 50.

8. Jared Diamond, "What Makes Countries Rich or Poor?," *New York Review of Books*, June 7, 2012. Accessed March 6, 2018, at: http://www.nybooks.com/articles/2012/06/07/what-makes-countries-rich-or-poor.

9. Jared Diamond, *Guns, Germs, and Steel: The Fates of Human Societies* (New York: W.W. Norton & Company, 1999).

10. Daron Acemoglu and James A. Robinson, *Why Nations Fail: The Origins of Power, Prosperity, and Poverty* (New York: Crown Business, 2012), 19.

11. Isabel V. Sawhill, *Generation Unbound: Drifting into Sex and Parenthood Without Marriage* (Washington, DC: The Brookings Institution, 2014), 78-79.

12. "Circles USA," Circles USA, accessed October 17, 2018, https://www.circlesusa.org.

Chapter Nine

1. Based on 2013 numbers: a population of 7.183 billion with a poverty rate of 10.7%.

2. Jonathan Tanner, "Ending World Poverty Is an Unrealistic Goal," *Guardian*, March 11, 2014, accessed October 15, 2018, https://www.theguardian.com/global-development-professionals-network/2014/mar/11/end-world-poverty-unrealistic-inequality.

3. O'Fallon's full statement of this right is as "the right to be developmentally at whatever stage one occupies as long as they aren't hurting anyone else." As will be seen in the discussion that follows, I separate the right to be where one is [developmentally] from the discussion of the appropriate responses to hurtful behaviors. Terri O'Fallon, "How Development Shapes Leadership, Systems, and Norms," June 2016, 14, unpublished paper provided to the author, October 18, 2018.

4. David T. Ellwood, *Poor Support: Poverty in the American Family* (New York: Basic Books, 1988), 11.

5. Abhijit V. Banerjee and Esther Duflo, *Poor Economics: A Radical Rethinking of the Way to Fight Poverty* (New York: PublicAffairs, 2011), 226-227.

6. "Health Equity," World Health Organization, accessed October 15, 2018, http://www.who.int/topics/health_equity/en/.

7. The use of the word "determinants" suggests the persistence of the Newtonian deterministic thinking described in Chapter 5.

8. Frederic Laloux proposes that street gangs are an organizational manifestation of the developmental stage captured by Loevinger's Self-Protective. As noted earlier, Lewis points to street gangs as a high point of social organization within

the "culture of poverty." Frederic Laloux, *Reinventing Organizations: A Guide to Creating Organizations Inspired by the Next Stage of Human Consciousness* (Brussels: Nelson Parker, 2014). Oscar Lewis, "The Culture of Poverty," *Scientific American* 215, no. 4 (October 1966).

9. Erik H. Erikson, *Insight and Responsibility: Lectures on the Ethical Implications of Psychoanalytic Insight* (New York: W.W. Norton & Company, 1964), 125-126.

10. Marshall B. Rosenberg, *Nonviolent Communication: A Language of Life* (Encinitas, CA: PuddleDancer Press, 2003), 148.

11. Abraham Joshua Heschel, *God in Search of Man: A Philosophy of Judaism* (New York: Farrar, Straus and Giroux, 1976).

12. Eric Meade, "What If We Loved the Poor?," *World Future Review*, Spring 2010.

13. Martin Luther King, Jr., *Stride Toward Freedom: The Montgomery Story* (New York: Harper & Brothers, Publishers, 1958), 212.

14. Karla McLaren, *The Language of Emotions: What Your Feelings Are Trying to Tell You* (Boulder, CO: Sounds True, 2010).

15. Ibid., 227.

Epilogue

1. Abraham Joshua Heschel, *God in Search of Man: A Philosophy of Judaism* (New York: Farrar, Straus and Giroux, 1976), 357.

2. Erik H. Erikson, *Insight and Responsibility: Lectures on the Ethical Implications of Psychoanalytic Insight* (New York: W.W. Norton & Company, 1964), 133.

3. Theodore Parker, *The Collected Works of Theodore Parker, Vol. 2: Ten Sermons of Religion*, ed. Frances Power Cobbe (London, Trübner & Co., 1879), 49.

4. James C. Riley, "Estimates of Regional and Global Life Expectancy, 1800-2001," *Population and Development Review* 31, no. 3 (September 2005): 537-543.

5. Max Roser, "Child Mortality," OurWorldInData.org, accessed October 15, 2018, https://ourworldindata.org/child-mortality.

6. UNESCO. *Education for All Global Monitoring Report*, accessed October 15, 2018, http://www.unesco.org/education/GMR2006/full/chapt8_eng.pdf.

CPSIA information can be obtained
at www.ICGtesting.com
Printed in the USA
LVHW041631140820
663221LV00004B/759